Getting Started with OAuth 2.0

Ryan Boyd

Beijing · Cambridge · Farnham · Köln · Sebastopol · Tokyo

Getting Started with OAuth 2.0

by Ryan Boyd

Published by O'Reilly Media, Inc., 1005 Gravenstein Highway North, Sebastopol, CA 95472.

O'Reilly books may be purchased for educational, business, or sales promotional use. Online editions are also available for most titles (*http://my.safaribooksonline.com*). For more information, contact our corporate/institutional sales department: (800) 998-9938 or *corporate@oreilly.com*.

Editors: Mike Loukides and Shawn Wallace
Production Editor: Teresa Elsey

Cover Designer: Karen Montgomery
Interior Designer: David Futato
Illustrator: Robert Romano

Revision History for the First Edition:

   2012-02-17   First release

See *http://oreilly.com/catalog/errata.csp?isbn=9781449311605* for release details.

ISBN: 978-1-449-31160-5

[LSI]

1329510994

Table of Contents

Preface

I've been working with web-based APIs since 1999, building SOAP-based web services for internal IT applications and helping thousands of developers using Google's REST-based APIs for Google Calendar, Picasa Web Albums, YouTube, and more. Each of these APIs has required authorization from users to act on their behalf. Developers using these Google APIs were initially required to use proprietary technologies like ClientLogin and AuthSub. If these same developers wanted to integrate with APIs provided by Yahoo!, they needed to use Yahoo!'s BBAuth. The use of these proprietary authorization technologies made it challenging to build applications using APIs from multiple providers.

The development of OAuth 1.0 reduced many of the headaches for developers and allowed them to use a single authorization technology across hundreds of APIs on the Web. However, OAuth 1.0 came with some challenges as well—cryptographic signatures and limited definition of how to use it for authorizing applications not using a server-to-server web application flow. I'm delighted that the standardization of OAuth 2.0 is nearly complete, as it provides an authorization protocol that's easy to use both for these types of applications and for a variety of other use cases.

Perhaps most exciting is the upcoming standardization of OpenID Connect—a protocol built on top of OAuth 2.0 to enable using the same identity to log in (authenticate) to multiple applications. While I've worked with hundreds of developers who have successfully built earlier versions of OpenID authentication into their web applications, it's rarely been a very smooth process. Just as OAuth 2.0 makes authorization easier for developers, OpenID Connect does the same for authentication.

I hope this book gives you the foundation knowledge you need to work with OAuth 2.0 and OpenID Connect as the next-generation authorization and authentication technologies for the Web.

Conventions Used in This Book

The following typographical conventions are used in this book:

Italic

Indicates new terms, URLs, email addresses, filenames, and file extensions.

`Constant width`

Used for program listings, as well as within paragraphs to refer to program elements such as variable or function names, databases, data types, environment variables, statements, and keywords.

`Constant width bold`

Shows commands or other text that should be typed literally by the user.

`Constant width italic`

Shows text that should be replaced with user-supplied values or by values determined by context.

 This icon signifies a tip, suggestion, or general note.

 This icon indicates a warning or caution.

Using Code Examples

This book is here to help you get your job done. In general, you may use the code in this book in your programs and documentation. You do not need to contact us for permission unless you're reproducing a significant portion of the code. For example, writing a program that uses several chunks of code from this book does not require permission. Selling or distributing a CD-ROM of examples from O'Reilly books does require permission. Answering a question by citing this book and quoting example code does not require permission. Incorporating a significant amount of example code from this book into your product's documentation does require permission.

We appreciate, but do not require, attribution. An attribution usually includes the title, author, publisher, and ISBN. For example: "*Getting Started with OAuth 2.0* by Ryan Boyd (O'Reilly). Copyright 2012 Ryan Boyd, 978-1-449-31160-5."

If you feel your use of code examples falls outside fair use or the permission given above, feel free to contact us at *permissions@oreilly.com*.

Safari® Books Online

Safari Books Online is an on-demand digital library that lets you easily search over 7,500 technology and creative reference books and videos to find the answers you need quickly.

With a subscription, you can read any page and watch any video from our library online. Read books on your cell phone and mobile devices. Access new titles before they are available for print, and get exclusive access to manuscripts in development and post feedback for the authors. Copy and paste code samples, organize your favorites, download chapters, bookmark key sections, create notes, print out pages, and benefit from tons of other time-saving features.

O'Reilly Media has uploaded this book to the Safari Books Online service. To have full digital access to this book and others on similar topics from O'Reilly and other publishers, sign up for free at *http://my.safaribooksonline.com*.

How to Contact Us

Please address comments and questions concerning this book to the publisher:

O'Reilly Media, Inc.
1005 Gravenstein Highway North
Sebastopol, CA 95472
800-998-9938 (in the United States or Canada)
707-829-0515 (international or local)
707-829-0104 (fax)

We have a web page for this book, where we list errata, examples, and any additional information. You can access this page at:

http://shop.oreilly.com/product/0636920021810.do

To comment or ask technical questions about this book, send email to:

bookquestions@oreilly.com

For more information about our books, courses, conferences, and news, see our website at *http://www.oreilly.com*.

Find us on Facebook: *http://facebook.com/oreilly*

Follow us on Twitter: *http://twitter.com/oreillymedia*

Watch us on YouTube: *http://www.youtube.com/oreillymedia*

Acknowledgments

I'd like to thank the identity and auth teams at Google for providing years of guidance and expertise, and most importantly Eric Sachs, Marius Scurtescu, and Breno de Medeiros for their review and feedback on this book. I also would like to thank my family, friends, and colleagues in Google's Developer Relations group for their constant support.

Of course, without the fantastic work of the OAuth spec authors and working groups, nobody would have a chance to use or write about OAuth.

CHAPTER 1

Introduction

How OAuth Was Born

In the movie *Ferris Bueller's Day Off*, a valet attendant takes a fully restored 1961 Ferrari out for a joyride. How do you prevent the same thing from happening to your brand-new Mustang? Some cars now come with special keys that allow the owner to provide limited authorization to valet attendants (or kids!) and prevent activities such as opening the trunk and driving at excessive speeds.

OAuth was created to solve the same core issue online.

When Google first released the Google Calendar API, it provided the ability for application developers to read and manipulate a user's Google Calendar. However, the only way for a user to provide delegated access was to give the application his or her account username and password, which the application would then use with Google's proprietary ClientLogin protocol.

Proprietary protocols like ClientLogin and standard protocols like HTTP Basic authentication resulted in both small and big applications requesting passwords from users to get access to their data. This wasn't affecting just desktop apps—applications all over the Web were prompting for credentials. Flickr, an online photo-sharing site, was one such application. Originally an independent company, Flickr was acquired by Yahoo! a few years after Google bought Blogger. The idea of Yahoo! asking for Google user passwords scared both firms, leading to the development of new proprietary protocols that tackled this problem on the Web.

With these new protocols, such as Google's AuthSub (see Figure 1-1) and Yahoo!'s BBAuth, an application would redirect users to an authorization page on the provider's site if the app needed access to user data. Users would log in to their accounts and grant access, and then the application would get a token to use for accessing the users' data.

While this solved some security issues, it also created costs for developers. Developers integrating with multiple major API providers had to learn and implement several web-based authorization protocols in their applications. Startups building new APIs

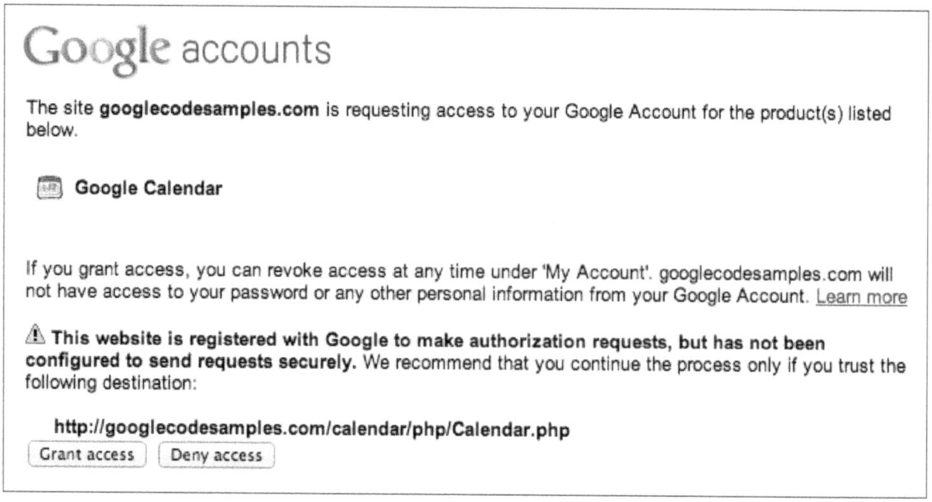

Figure 1-1. Google's AuthSub approval screen, asking users for permission for their Google Calendar

were not comfortable implementing the proprietary auth schemes, nor developing their own custom schemes, which might introduce security vulnerabilities. Instead, these startups and major API providers decided that they needed to create a standard protocol to improve consistency for these web-based authorization flows.

Why Developers Should Care About OAuth

With wide adoption of collaboration platforms and social networks, application developers have the opportunity to connect users with their data wherever they are on the Web. Connecting users with their data results in improved day-to-day efficiency by eliminating data silos and also allows developers to differentiate their applications from the competition.

OAuth provides the ability for these applications to access a user's data securely, without requiring the user to take the scary step of handing over an account password.

Types of functionality provided by OAuth-enabled APIs include the following:

- Getting access to a user's *social graph* — their Facebook friends, people they're following on Twitter, or their Google Contacts
- *Sharing* information about a user's activities on your site by posting to their Facebook wall or Twitter stream
- Accessing a user's Google Docs or Dropbox account to *store data* in their online filesystem of choice
- Integrating business applications with one another to drive smarter decisions by *mashing up* multiple data sources such as a Salesforce CRM and TripIt travel plan

In order to access or update private data via each of these APIs, an application needs to be delegated access by the owner of the data. Each of these APIs, and over 300 more around the Web (according to Programmable Web in February 2012), support OAuth for getting access.

Having a common protocol for handling API authorization greatly improves the developer experience because it lessens the learning curve required to integrate with a new API. At the same time, an authorization standard creates more confidence in the security of APIs because the standard has been vetted by a large community.

Why Don't These APIs Just Use Passwords for Authorization?

Usernames and passwords are typically the lowest common denominator for authentication and authorization on the Web. They are used for HTTP Basic and HTTP Digest authentication and on countless login pages. However, asking a user for their password has a number of side effects:

Trust
A user may not trust providing their password to your application.

Decreased user sensitivity to phishing
Even if the user is comfortable providing their password to your application, making the user comfortable doing this around the Web can have negative long-term effects, such as making phishing scams more effective.

Expanded access and risk
When the user provides their password to your application, you get access to not only the data your application needs, but all other data in the user's account. The application has an obligation to its users to securely store these passwords and prevent them from leaking. Many developers do not want the risk exposure of having this additional responsibility.

Limited reliability
When a user changes their password, your application no longer has access to their data.

Revocation challenges
The only way a user can revoke access to your application is by changing their password, which also revokes access to all other apps.

Passwords become required
When an API provider supports federated authentication mechanisms such as OpenID or SAML (see "Federated Authentication" on page 4), users may not have passwords on their accounts. This makes it impossible for those users to use applications powered by the API.

Difficulty implementing stronger authentication
> If an API provider requires passwords for API authentication, it becomes challenging to improve account security with technologies like CAPTCHAs or multifactor authentication (such as one-time password tokens).

Terminology

In order to understand OAuth, it's important to first understand the relevant terminology. We'll introduce some key terms up front, and then discuss additional terms throughout the book.

Authentication

Authentication is the process of verifying the identity of a user—knowing that the user is who they claim to be.

In the real world, when a police officer asks for your identification, she's verifying your identity by ensuring that the picture on your identification matches your likeness.

On desktop computers and on the Web, authentication is about knowing that the user at the keyboard is the owner of the account. Authentication is typically performed by asking a user for a username and password. The username represents the user's claimed identity, and the software application assumes that if the user provides the correct password that they are indeed that user.

Federated Authentication

Although many applications have their own system of accounts (including usernames and passwords), some applications rely on other services to verify the identity of users. This is called federated authentication.

In a corporate IT environment, applications may trust an Active Directory server, a LDAP server, or a SAML provider to authenticate users.

On the Web, applications often trust OpenID providers (such as Google or Yahoo!) to handle the authentication of users. There are many benefits to federation for both application developers and users. OpenID is the most common open web protocol for handling federated authentication.

Although OpenID has been used on the Web for many years, we'll discuss only OpenID Connect, which is the next-generation version of OpenID based on OAuth 2.0.

Authorization

Authorization is the process of verifying that a user has the right to perform some action, such as reading a document or accessing an email account. This typically first requires valid identification of the user (authentication) in order to check whether the actual user is authorized.

When a police officer pulls over your car for speeding, she first authenticates you using your driver's license (to verify your identity) and then checks the license (expiration date, restrictions, etc.) to ensure you're authorized to drive.

The same process happens online — a web application first verifies your identity by logging you in, and then it ensures that you access only the data and services you're allowed to, typically by checking an access control list for each operation.

Delegated Authorization

Delegated authorization is granting access to another person or application to perform actions on your behalf.

When you drive your car to a classy hotel, they may offer valet parking. You then authorize the valet attendant to drive your car by handing him the key in order to let him perform actions on your behalf.

OAuth works similarly—a user grants access to an application to perform actions on the user's behalf and the application can only perform the authorized actions.

Roles

There are several key actors in the OAuth protocol flows:

Resource server
> The server hosting user-owned resources that are protected by OAuth. This is typically an API provider that holds and protects data such as photos, videos, calendars, or contacts.

Resource owner
> Typically the user of an application, the resource owner has the ability to grant access to their own data hosted on the resource server.

Client
> An application making API requests to perform actions on protected resources on behalf of the resource owner and with its authorization.

Authorization server
> The authorization server gets consent from the resource owner and issues access tokens to clients for accessing protected resources hosted by a resource server. Smaller API providers may use the same application and URL space for both the authorization server and resource server.

The Great Debate over Signatures

OAuth 1.0 required cryptographic signatures be sent with each API request to verify the identity and authorization of the client. Cryptography is challenging for the casual developer to grasp and also challenging for even highly skilled engineers to master. This led to plenty of developer frustration and, presumably, less adoption of APIs than could have been achieved with an easier authorization protocol.

When OAuth 1.0 was developed in 2007, it was decided that cryptographic signatures were necessary to support the security of APIs. At the time, many top API providers hosted their APIs at vanilla HTTP endpoints, without SSL/TLS protection. Over the years, SSL/TLS became a more common way of protecting APIs and the need for signatures decreased in the eyes of some members of the security community.

Combining the perception of low API adoption due to the complexity of cryptography in OAuth 1.0 and the greater prevalence of SSL/TLS support for APIs led to the development of the OAuth Web Resource Authorization Profiles (WRAP) specification. OAuth WRAP is the predecessor to OAuth 2.0—it eliminated the complex signature requirements and introduced the use of *bearer* tokens.

Even as OAuth 2.0 nears finalization in the standards community, there remains some strong individual opposition to not requiring the use of signatures, including by Eran Hammer-Lahav, the editor of the specification. Eran has written a blog post titled OAuth 2.0 (without Signatures) Is Bad for the Web (*http://hueniverse.com/2010/09/oauth-2-0-without-signatures-is-bad-for-the-web/*), in which he acknowledges the complexity of signatures for some developers but defends their value. He mainly points out that removing signatures from OAuth 2.0 makes it easy for developers to make mistakes and accidentally send their credentials to a malicious API endpoint, which can then abuse these credentials to make additional requests because they're not protected by a signature. While he argues that this isn't likely today, he does believe it will become more critical as automated discovery is added for API and OAuth endpoints. Others identify cryptographic signatures as a feature that allows for greater confidence in the origin of API requests as the requests pass through multitiered architectures.

Engineers often have to strike a delicate balance between security and usability, and this case is no different.

Mitigating Concerns with Bearer Tokens

One of the primary concerns with the elimination of signatures is that developers will not properly verify SSL/TLS certificate chains when making requests to the authorization and resource servers. This is required by the specification and addressed in the OAuth 2.0 threat model document (*http://tools.ietf.org/html/draft-ietf-oauth-v2-threat model-00#section-5.1.2*), but the ease of disabling proper certificate and certificate authority validation in popular libraries, combined with the difficulty of fixing issues associated with it, has resulted in many developers taking shortcuts that threaten the security of their applications.

When implementing OAuth 2.0, calling any APIs, or using a library, you should verify that it properly handles SSL/TLS certificate chain validation by doing the following things:

- Checking that the hostname on the certificate returned by the server matches the hostname in the URL being accessed
- Verifying each certificate in the chain properly chains up to a valid and trusted certificate authority (CA)
- Ensuring that the certificate authority bundle on your server is secure and not able to be modified by potential attackers

Signing Your OAuth 2.0 Requests

The MAC Access Authentication (*http://tools.ietf.org/html/draft-ietf-oauth-v2-http -mac-00*) specification defines how clients can sign their OAuth 2.0 requests when signatures are supported or required by the API provider.

Author's Note: If you're thinking *MAC* only refers to a type of computer, you can understand why signatures are hard for many developers! You might want to find a good book on cryptography.

Getting the key

In order to sign requests using MAC authentication, the client must first get a MAC key. This can be issued by the OAuth authorization server. In this case, the key is returned each time an access_token is returned by the authorization server. This MAC key must be for use in either the hmac-sha-1 or hmac-sha-256 algorithms. Alternatively, the MAC key can be issued in an out-of-band process, such as when the developer registers their application with the API provider. Regardless of how the key is issued, it must always be issued over a secure SSL/TLS channel and must be kept confidential.

Making API requests

When connecting to OAuth-enabled APIs that require signatures, each API request must include a MAC signature in the Authorization header of the request. The process of generating this signature involves creating a normalized request string (nonce, HTTP method, request URI, host, port, optional body hash, etc.) and performing a cryptographic signature. It is highly recommended that developers use a prebuilt library to handle OAuth MAC signing if needed. If you need to build your own implementation, please see the specification (*http://tools.ietf.org/html/draft-ietf-oauth-v2-http-mac-00 #section-3*), as the details are out of scope for this book.

Developer and Application Registration

OAuth requires that applications register with the authorization server so that API requests are able to be properly identified. While the protocol allows for registration using automated means, most API providers require manual registration via filling out a form on their developer websites.

At the time of this writing

- Google requires you to register your client by visiting its APIs Console (*http://code .google.com/apis/console*), as shown in Figure 1-2.
- Microsoft Windows Live requires you to register your client using its application management site (*https://manage.dev.live.com/*).
- Facebook requires you to register your client on the Facebook Developers site (*https://developers.facebook.com/apps*).

Figure 1-2. Google's APIs Console for OAuth app registration

As an example, the following information is required to register an OAuth client with Google via their APIs Console:

- Google Account
- Product Name
- Product Logo (optional)
- Website URL used for Redirect URIs (for web applications only)

After registration is complete, the developer is issued client credentials:

Client ID
    Specified as `client_id` when interacting with the resource server

Client Secret

    Specified as `client_secret` when exchanging an authorization code for an access token and refreshing access tokens using the server-side Web Application Flow (see Figure 7-1).

Why Is Registration Necessary?

Registration enables the application developer to obtain client credentials, which are used to authenticate requests made to the authorization server. These credentials are critical in protecting the authenticity of requests when performing operations such as exchanging authorization codes for access tokens and refreshing access tokens (as described in Chapter 2).

Registration also gives the API provider information to improve the user experience during the authorization process. When presenting an application's request for data access to the user, the API provider will often display the name and logo of the application.

See Figure 2-3 for an example of how Google uses the registration information on the approval screen.

Client Profiles, Access Tokens, and Authorization Flows

The first version of OAuth was designed primarily to handle API authorization for classic client-server web applications. The specification did not define how to handle authorization in mobile applications, desktop applications, JavaScript applications, browser extensions, or other situations. While each of these types of apps have been written using OAuth 1.0, the method of implementation is inconsistent and often suboptimal, as the protocol wasn't designed for these cases.

OAuth 2.0 was architected with this variety of use cases in mind.

Client Profiles

OAuth 2.0 defines several important *client profiles*:

Server-side web application
    An OAuth client running on a web server. The web application is accessed by a resource owner (user) and the application makes the appropriate API calls using a server-side programming language. The user has no access to the OAuth client secret or any access tokens issued by the authorization server.

Client-side application running in a web browser
    An OAuth client running in a user's web browser, where the client has access to the application code and/or API requests. The application could be distributed as JavaScript included in a web page, as a browser extension, or using a plug-in tech-

nology such as Flash. The OAuth credentials are not trusted to be kept confidential from the resource owner, so some API providers won't issue client secrets for applications using this profile.

Native application
> An OAuth client which is very similar to the client-side application, as the credentials are not trusted to be kept confidential. However, since it's an installed application, it may not have access to the full capabilities of a web browser.

Access Tokens

Although signature-based MAC Access Authentication was mentioned earlier, most OAuth 2.0 authorized APIs require only bearer tokens to make authorized requests. Bearer tokens are a type of access token whereby simple possession of the token values provides access to protected resources. No additional information, such as a cryptographic key, is needed to make API calls.

Whether you're building a server-side web application, client-side web application, or a native application, the end goal of using OAuth is the same: you're trying to obtain an OAuth access token that your application can use to perform API requests on behalf of a user or the application itself.

After obtaining an access token, the token can be sent along with your requests in one of several ways. The preferred method of authorizing requests is by sending the access token in a HTTP `Authorization` header:

```
GET /tasks/v1/lists/@default/tasks HTTP/1.1
Host: www.googleapis.com
Authorization: Bearer ya29.AHES6ZSzX
```

The `Authorization` header is the preferred mechanism because

- The header is rarely logged by proxy servers and web server access logs.
- The header is almost never cached.
- The header doesn't get stored in the browser cache when making requests from the client.

While the other mechanisms are defined in the specification, API providers are not required to implement any of these additional methods, so your mileage will vary:

Query parameter
> Including the `access_token` as a URL query parameter is useful for debugging and when libraries make it difficult to modify the `Authorization` header. This mechanism is also valuable when using the client-side flow and sending a token in a JSONP request. For example,
>
> ```
> https://www.googleapis.com/tasks/v1/lists/@default/tasks?
> callback=outputTasks&access_token=ya29.AHES6ZThOOgsAn4
> ```

Form-encoded body parameter
> This is a fallback mechanism for when an application cannot modify the `Authori zation` header on requests. It is only to be used when a HTTP body would normally be sent and can then be added as an additional form parameter in an `application/ x-www-form-urlencoded` body. This mechanism is not supported by the Google Tasks API.

Authorization Flows

Each of the client profiles needs to be accommodated with an appropriate protocol flow for obtaining authorization from the resource owner for access to their data. The core OAuth 2.0 protocol defines four primary "grant types" used for obtaining authorization and also defines an extension mechanism for enabling additional grant types.

Authorization code
> This grant type is most appropriate for server-side web applications. After the resource owner has authorized access to their data, they are redirected back to the web application with an authorization code as a query parameter in the URL. This code must be exchanged for an access token by the client application. This exchange is done server-to-server and requires both the `client_id` and `cli ent_secret`, preventing even the resource owner from obtaining the access token. This grant type also allows for long-lived access to an API by using refresh tokens.

Implicit grant for browser-based client-side applications
> The implicit grant is the most simplistic of all flows, and is optimized for client-side web applications running in a browser. The resource owner grants access to the application, and a new access token is immediately minted and passed back to the application using a #hash fragment in the URL. The application can immediately extract the access token from the hash fragment (using JavaScript) and make API requests. This grant type does not require the intermediary "authorization code," but it also doesn't make available refresh tokens for long-lived access.

Resource owner password-based grant
> This grant type enables a resource owner's username and password to be exchanged for an OAuth access token. It is used for only highly-trusted clients, such as a mobile application written by the API provider. While the user's password is still exposed to the client, it does not need to be stored on the device. After the initial authentication, only the OAuth token needs to be stored. Because the password is not stored, the user can revoke access to the app without changing the password, and the token is scoped to a limited set of data, so this grant type still provides enhanced security over traditional username/password authentication.

Client credentials
> The client credentials grant type allows an application to obtain an access token for resources owned by the client or when authorization has been "previously arranged with an authorization server." This grant type is appropriate for applica-

tions that need to access APIs, such as storage services or databases, on behalf of themselves rather than on behalf of a specific user.

These additional flows are defined outside of the core spec:

Device profile

The device profile was created to enable OAuth to be used on devices that do not have built-in web browsers or have limited input options—such as a game console or electronic photo frame. The user typically initiates the flow on the device and is then told to use a computer to access a website and approve access for the device by typing in an authorization code displayed in the device. Facebook has a great example of this flow (*http://oauth-device-demo.appspot.com/*) referenced in its documentation (*http://developers.facebook.com/docs/authentication/devices/*).

SAML bearer assertion profile

This profile enables exchanging SAML 2.0 assertion for an OAuth access token. This is useful in enterprise environments that already have SAML authorization servers set up to control application and data access.

CHAPTER 2

Server-Side Web Application Flow

In the Web Application flow (also known as the Authorization Code flow), the resource owner is first redirected by the application to the OAuth authorization server at the API provider. The authorization server checks to see if the user has an active session. If she does, the authorization server prompts her for access to the requested data. After she grants access, she is redirected back to the web application and an authorization code is included in the URL as the `code` query parameter:

```
http://www.example.com/oauth_callback?code=ABC1234
```

Because the `code` is passed as a query parameter, the web browser sends it along to the web server that is acting as the OAuth client. This authorization code is then exchanged for an access token using a server-to-server call from the application to the authorization server. This access token is used by the client to make API calls.

Sound confusing? Figure 2-1 shows the flow step-by-step, based on a diagram from the specification.

When Should the Authorization Code Flow Be Used?

The Authorization Code flow should be used when

- Long-lived access is required.
- The OAuth client is a web application server.
- Accountability for API calls is very important and the OAuth token shouldn't be leaked to the browser, where the user may have access to it.

Security Properties

The Authorization Code flow does not expose the access token to the resource owner's browser. Instead, authorization is accomplished using an intermediary "authorization code" that is passed through the browser. This `code` must be exchanged for an access

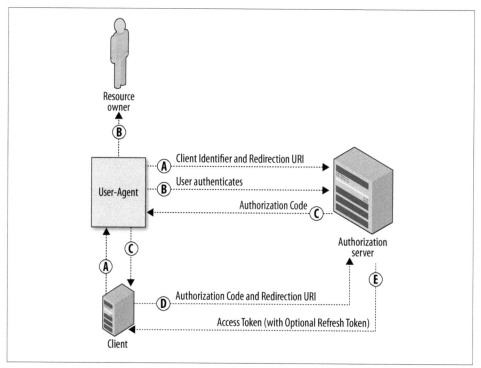

Figure 2-1. Server-side Web Application flow: Step-by-step

token before calls can be made to protected APIs. The exchange process only succeeds if a correct `client_secret` is passed with the request, ensuring confidentiality of the access token as long as client security is maintained. Unlike with the Implicit flow described in Chapter 3, this confidentiality also extends to the resource owner, meaning API requests made with the access token are directly attributable to the client and its developers. Perhaps most importantly—because the access token is never sent through the browser— there is less risk that the access token will be leaked to malicious code through browser history, referer headers, JavaScript, and the like.

Although there is less chance of the access token leaking because it's not exposed to the browser, many applications using this flow will store long-lived refresh tokens in the application's database or key store to enable "offline" access to data. There is additional risk when an application requires long-lived offline access to data, as this creates a single point of compromise for accessing data belonging to many users. This doesn't exist with other flows, such as the flow for client-side web applications (see Chapter 3). Even with this additional risk, many websites will choose to use "offline" data access because their application architecture makes it difficult to interact with the user's browser to obtain new access tokens.

User Experience

Let's take an example of a payroll application. The payroll application wants access to update a manager's task list to remind the manager to approve timesheets. By placing these reminders in the manager's task list, which the manager uses every day, it's much more likely that employees will get paid on time, reducing the number of angry employees and time-consuming calls to the HR department.

The user experience in the most common case is very simple:

1. Payroll application lets the manager know that it's asking for access to modify her tasks, and redirects her over to the task list app's OAuth authorization server (see Figure 2-2).
2. The OAuth authorization server used by the task list app's API prompts the user to grant permission for the payroll application to update her tasks (see Figure 2-3).
3. After the user has approved, she is redirected back to the payroll application, which now has access to the tasks (see Figure 2-4).

Step-by-Step

After registering your app (see "Developer and Application Registration" on page 8) with the API provider and obtaining an OAuth client ID and client secret, it's time to start writing code! Let's go through each step of the flow and show how the protocol works. We'll use PHP as the example programming language and the Google Tasks API (*http://code.google.com/apis/tasks/*) along with Google's OAuth 2.0 authorization server (*http://code.google.com/apis/accounts/docs/OAuth2.html*).

Although we'll write the PHP code using the raw OAuth protocol, many API providers distribute client libraries for accessing their services. These libraries abstract away some of the details of implementing OAuth 2.0 and make it easier for developers. You can find information on Google's PHP library, which works with Google Tasks, Google+, and many other Google APIs, at code.google.com (*http://code.google.com/p/google-api -php-client/wiki/OAuth2*).

Step 1: Let the user know what you're doing and request authorization

Since the OAuth flow involves directing your users to the website of the API provider to obtain authorization, it's a best practice to let them know in advance what will happen. You can do this by displaying a message, along with a link (the "Add tasks to your Google Tasks" link in Figure 2-2).

After the user initiates the flow, your application will need to send the user's browser to the OAuth authorization page (as seen in Figure 2-3). This can be done either by sending the main browser window directly to the authorization endpoint or by creating a pop up. On this page, the API provider will present the user with a request to approve

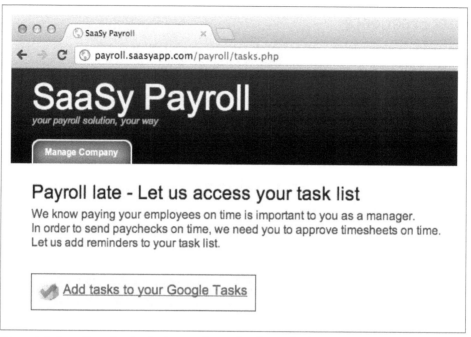

Figure 2-2. Payroll application letting user know they'll soon be directed over to the task list app's approval screen.

Figure 2-3. OAuth authorization server asking user if it's OK to let the payroll application access his or her tasks.

the application's ability to access the user's data. Of course, the user needs to already be signed in to the API provider, or they will be prompted to authenticate before being asked to grant access to their data.

Figure 2-4. Payroll app thanking the user for access, and reminding them what they'll use the access to enable.

You can find the URL for the OAuth authorization endpoint in the API provider's documentation. For Google Tasks (and all other Google APIs using OAuth 2.0), the authorization endpoint is at

```
https://accounts.google.com/o/oauth2/auth
```

You will need to specify a few query parameters with this link:

client_id
> The value provided to you when you registered your application.

redirect_uri
> The location the user should be returned to after they approve access for your app. For this example, the application will use *https://payroll.saasyapp.com/oauth_response.php*. The value used for the `redirect_uri` typically needs to be registered in advance with the provider.

scope
> The data your application is requesting access to. This is typically specified as a list of space-delimited strings, though Facebook uses comma-delimited strings. Valid values for the `scope` should be included in the API provider documentation. For Google Tasks, the `scope` is `https://www.googleapis.com/auth/tasks`. If an application also needed access to Google Docs, it would specify a `scope` value of `https://www.googleapis.com/auth/tasks https://docs.google.com/feeds`.

response_type

> code for the server-side Web Application flow, indicating that an authorization
> code will be returned to the application after the user approves the authorization
> request.

state

> A unique value used by your application in order to prevent cross-site request
> forgery (CSRF) attacks on your implementation. The value should be a random
> unique string for this particular request, unguessable and kept secret in the client
> (perhaps in a server-side session).

Here's what the PHP code may look like:

```php
<?php
session_start();

// Generate random value for use as the 'state'. Mitigates
// risk of CSRF attacks when this value is verified against the
// value returned from the OAuth provider with the authorization
// code.
$_SESSION['state'] = rand(0,999999999);

$authorizationUrlBase = 'https://accounts.google.com/o/oauth2/auth';
$redirectUriPath = '/oauth2callback.php';

// For example only.  A valid value for client_id needs to be obtained
// for your environment from the Google APIs Console at
// http://code.google.com/apis/console.
$queryParams = array(
  'client_id' => '240195362.apps.googleusercontent.com',
  'redirect_uri' => (isset($_SERVER['HTTPS'])?'https://':'http://') .
                    $_SERVER['HTTP_HOST'] . $redirectUriPath,
  'scope' => 'https://www.googleapis.com/auth/tasks',
  'response_type' => 'code',
  'state' => $_SESSION['state'],
  'approval_prompt' => 'force', // always request user consent
  'access_type' => 'offline' // obtain a refresh token
);

$goToUrl = $authorizationUrlBase . '?' . http_build_query($queryParams);

// Output a webpage directing users to the $goToUrl after
// they click a "Let's Go" button
include 'access_request_template.php';
?>
```

In addition to the standard OAuth query parameters, you'll notice we've included a
few which are specific to Google's implementation (*http://code.google.com/apis/ac
counts/docs/OAuth2WebServer.html#formingtheurl*):

approval_prompt

> Use `force` to indicate that we want the user prompted for approval each time the user visits the application. You can also use `auto` to indicate that the user will only see the approval request the first time this application requires it.

access_type

> Use `offline` to indicate that the application needs access to user data while the user is not at the keyboard. This results in a refresh token being issued when the user explicitly approves granting access to this app. If `online` is used, no refresh token will be issued.

Some enterprise API providers have special provisions to handle auto-approval of OAuth 2.0 grants for an individual user if an IT administrator of the user's organization has previously approved access for an application. In this scenario, the application will redirect the user's browser to the authorization server, but the user will never be prompted to approve access. Instead, the user will be immediately redirected back to the application with an authorization code, as described below in "Step 2: Exchange authorization code for an access token" on page 20. Salesforce provides this option as "no user approval required" (*https://login.salesforce.com/help/doc/en/remoteaccess _define.htm*) on their control panel page to define Remote Access Applications.

Error handling

If all request parameters are valid and the user approves the data access request, the user will be redirected back to the application at the URL specified as the `redirect_uri`.

However, if one of the request parameters is invalid, an error condition exists. If there is an issue with the `redirect_uri`, `client_id`, or other request information, the authorization server should present an error message to the user and not redirect the user back to the application.

In the case that the user (or authorization server) denies the access request, an error response will be generated, and the user will be redirected to the `redirect_uri` with a query parameter called `error` indicating the type of error as `access_denied`. Additionally, the server can include an `error_description` message and/or an `error_uri` indicating the URL of a web page containing more information about the error.

While `access_denied` is the most likely error response your application will need to handle, there are other error types defined in the OAuth 2.0 specification as well:

`invalid_request`

> The request is missing a required parameter, includes an unsupported parameter value, or is otherwise malformed.

`unauthorized_client`

> The client is not authorized to request an authorization code using this method.

unsupported_response_type

> The authorization server does not support obtaining an authorization code using this method.

invalid_scope

> The requested scope is invalid, unknown, or malformed.

server_error

> The authorization server encountered an unexpected condition that prevented it from fulfilling the request.

temporarily_unavailable

> The authorization server is currently unable to handle the request because of a temporary overloading or maintenance of the server.

Step 2: Exchange authorization code for an access token

In the case that no error occurs during the approval process, the authorization server will redirect the user back to the application at the URL specified as the redirect_uri. In this example, the user will be redirected back to https://payroll.saasyapp.com/oauth2callback.

When the user has granted access, two query parameters will be included by the authorization server in the redirect back to the web application:

code

> The authorization code, indicating that the user has approved the request for access

state

> The value of the state parameter passed in the initial request to the authorization server

The state value should be compared against the value generated in Step 1 above. If the values do not match, it's possible a malicious user is attempting to perform a cross-site request forgery attack on the application, so the OAuth flow should not be continued.

Take, for example,

```
https://payroll.saasyapp.com/oauth2callback?
code=AB231DEF2134123kj89&state=987d43e51a262f
```

The application needs to exchange the code for an OAuth access token to make API requests. If you're using a client library for OAuth, this exchange will typically happen behind the scenes by the library. However, if you're not using a library, you'll need to make a HTTP POST request to the token endpoint. The following parameters need to be passed in the request:

code

> The authorization code passed to the application

redirect_uri
> The location registered and used in the initial request to the authorization endpoint

grant_type
> The value `authorization_code`, indicating that you're exchanging an authorization code for an access token

This HTTP POST needs to be authenticated using the `client_id` and `client_secret` obtained during application registration. There are two primary ways to handle the authentication of the request defined in the specification: include a HTTP Basic `Author ization` header (with the `client_id` as the username, and the `client_secret` as the password) or include the `client_id` and `client_secret` as additional HTTP POST parameters.

A typical `Authorization` header looks like this:

```
Authorization: Basic
MDAwMDAwMDAONzU1REUOMzpVRWhrTDRzTmVOOFlhbG5OUHhnUjhaTWtpVU1nWWlJNg==
```

Because using HTTP Basic access authentication was a later addition to the OAuth 2.0 specifications, it is not yet supported by many providers. Instead, the HTTP POST parameter mechanism must be used. The following additional POST parameters must be passed alongside the `code` and `state`:

client_id
> The value provided to you when you registered your application

client_secret
> The confidential secret provided to you when you registered your application

If the request is properly authenticated and the other parameters are valid, the authorization server will issue and return an OAuth access token in a JSON-encoded response:

access_token
> A token that can be used to authorize API requests

token_type
> The type of access token issued, often "bearer," but the set of potential values is extensible

The access token may be time-limited, in which case some additional information may be returned:

expires_in
> The remaining lifetime of the access token, in seconds

refresh_token
> A token that can be used to acquire a new access token after the current one expires

The JSON-encoded response looks like this:

```
{
  "access_token" : "ya29.AHES6ZSzX",
```

```
  "token_type" : "Bearer",
  "expires_in" : 3600,
  "refresh_token" : "1/iQI98wWFfJNFWIzs5EDDrSiYewe3dFqt5vIV-9ibT9k"
}
```

 Because the OAuth specification is still in development, some API providers who haven't caught up with the latest specification may format
their responses differently. Facebook, for instance, returns a form-encoded (& delimited) response.

Here's example code for exchanging the authorization code for an access token in PHP:

```php
<?php
session_start();
include 'http_client.inc';

$code = $_GET['code'];
$state = $_GET['state'];

// Verify the 'state' value is the same random value we created
// when initiating the authorization request.
if ((! is_numeric($state)) || ($state != $_SESSION['state'])) {
  throw new Exception('Error validating state.  Possible CSRF.');
}

$accessTokenExchangeUrl = 'https://accounts.google.com/o/oauth2/token';
$redirectUriPath = '/oauth2callback.php';

// For example only.  Valid values for client_id and client_secret
// need to be obtained for your environment from the Google APIs
// Console at http://code.google.com/apis/console.
// Also, these values should not be hard-coded in a production application.
// Instead, they should be loaded in from a configuration file or secure keystore.
$accessTokenExchangeParams = array(
  'client_id' => '240195362.apps.googleusercontent.com',
  'client_secret' => 'hBMLD98Zi4wiqmiwmqDq',
  'grant_type' => 'authorization_code',
  'code' => $code,
  'redirect_uri' => (isset($_SERVER['HTTPS'])?'https://':'http://') .
                    $_SERVER['HTTP_HOST'] . $redirectUriPath
);

$httpClient = new HttpClient();
$responseJson = $httpClient->postData(
    $accessTokenExchangeUrl,
    $accessTokenExchangeParams);
$responseArray = json_decode($responseJson, TRUE);

$accessToken = $responseArray['access_token'];
$expiresIn = $responseArray['expires_in'];
$refreshToken = $responseArray['refresh_token'];

$_SESSION['access_token'] = $accessToken;
```

```
// Storing refresh token in the session, and using approval_prompt=force for
// simplicity. Typically the fresh token would be stored in a server-side database
// and associated with the user's account. This would eliminate the need for
// prompting the user for approval each time.
$_SESSION['refresh_token'] = $refreshToken;

header('Location: /get_data.php');
?>
```

Now that the app has an access token, the application can respond to the user to thank them for granting authorization, and remind them what features the access will enable. The application can now access the APIs directly through the lifetime of the access token or until the access is revoked. In the case a refresh token is provided, the application can continue to access the APIs offline without user interaction.

The access token and the refresh token should be kept secret at all times and they should not be exposed to any user, including the resource owner. Typically the refresh token is stored securely in a server-side database, associated with the user account. Access tokens can also be stored in a database, but they may also be cached in a server-side session to improve performance.

Why both access tokens and refresh tokens?

Some developers don't understand the need for both short-lived access tokens and long-lived refresh tokens. Having both token types improves security and performance, especially for large-scale API providers with many APIs and a central OAuth authorization service.

OAuth 2.0 typically uses bearer tokens (without signatures in API requests), so the compromise of a protected API service could allow an attacker to see the access tokens received from clients. An OAuth grant may provide an application access to multiple different APIs (scopes) for a user, such as the user's contacts and the user's calendars. This could allow an attacker access to not only the compromised service, but other services as well. Having only time-limited access tokens accessible to API services (and not long-lived refresh tokens) reduces the potential impact of an attack.

When an API service receives an access token from a client, it needs to ensure that it's valid for accessing the requested data. If the token is an opaque string, it determines the validity by making an internal request to the API service's OAuth authorization service or a database lookup. This can introduce latency to API requests, so some API providers instead of OAuth use access tokens, which are signed or encrypted strings and are able to be verified less expensively.

One of the key benefits of an authorization protocol like OAuth is the ability for users to revoke access they previously granted to applications. At large-scale providers, this revocation typically is handled by a central OAuth authorization service that handles requests for many APIs. If the API services are independently verifying the access tokens using cryptography without database lookups or calls to the central service, the services won't know when access for a client has been revoked. Thus it is important to keep the lifespan of the access tokens short so they do not remain valid for too long after the client's access is revoked.

Step 3: Call the API

The next step is retrieving and updating the user's tasks. Many API providers implementing OAuth 2.0 use *bearer* tokens. This means that the application can authorize API requests simply by including the OAuth access token in the requests, without the need for cryptographic signatures.

The preferred way of authorizing requests is by sending the access token in a HTTP `Authorization` header, as discussed in Chapter 1.

Here's an example of using the `Authorization` header method of making an authorized API call to retrieve a user's tasks in Google Tasks. Note that this code is again using a custom `HttpClient` class to implement the underlying calls to the `curl` library:

```php
<?php
session_start();
require_once 'http_client.inc';

$tasksUrl = 'https://www.googleapis.com/tasks/v1/lists/@default/tasks';

// The value for $accessToken would typically be stored in a
// server-side PHP session bound to the active user.  The value of the
// access token can be any string. Google uses values similar to:
// 'ya29.AHES6ZS_2G4-VuLO41LOGpFJqHOwGfGSR'.
$accessToken = $_SESSION['access_token'];

// Recommended approach for an OAuth 2 authorized request is to
// use a HTTP Authorization header
$httpClient = new HttpClient();
$headers = array(
  'Authorization: Bearer ' . $accessToken);

// Alternative to using the Authorization header would be appending
// the OAuth token to the URL as a query parameter
// $tasksUrl .= '?access_token=' . urlencode($accessToken);

$response = $httpClient->getData($tasksUrl, $headers);
$responseArray = json_decode($response, TRUE);

foreach ($responseArray["items"] as $item) {
  echo '<li>' . $item['title'] . "</li>\n";
}
?>
```

While this sample code specifically demonstrates calling the Google Tasks API, similar code could be used to authorize requests of any API supporting recent versions of the draft specification. Simply replace the values of `$tasksUrl` and `$accessToken`.

Error handling

When making API calls using the OAuth 2.0 access token, you may encounter errors if the access token is no longer valid because the token expired or was revoked. In this case, you should get a HTTP 4xx error. Depending on the individual API, the detailed error description will be communicated differently.

In addition to the 4xx error code, the latest version of the OAuth bearer token specification also requires that the HTTP `WWW-Authenticate` response header be included when credentials are not included in the request or the access token provided does not enable access to the requested API resource. This header may include additional details on the error encountered.

Here's an example response from the specification, indicating that an expired OAuth access token was passed to the app:

```
HTTP/1.1 401 Unauthorized
WWW-Authenticate: Bearer realm="example",
                  error="invalid_token",
                  error_description="The access token expired"
```

Valid error codes include: `invalid_request`, `invalid_token`, and `insufficient_scope`.

Because the use of the `WWW-Authenticate` header was a late addition to the spec, it may not be implemented by all of your favorite API providers.

When Facebook encounters an error with the token, it returns a HTTP 400 status code and includes the following JSON object in the body of the response:

```
{
    "error": {
       "type": "OAuthException",
       "message": "Error validating access token."
    }
}
```

Here's an example response resulting from the use of an expired access token with one of Google's newer APIs:

```
{
 "error": {
  "errors": [
   {
    "domain": "global",
    "reason": "authError",
    "message": "Invalid Credentials",
    "locationType": "header",
    "location": "Authorization"
   }
  ],
  "code": 401,
  "message": "Invalid Credentials"
 }
}
```

Step 4a: Refresh the access token

When an authorization code is exchanged for an access token, many API providers will issue short-lived access tokens even if they support long-lived "offline" access to their APIs. Although these access tokens have a limited lifespan, two additional parameters may be included in the response to enable long-lived access: expires_in and refresh_token.

If included in the response, expires_in indicates the remaining lifetime of the access_token, specified in seconds. When the access token expires, the refresh_token parameter can be used to obtain a new access token.

If trying to optimize for latency in your application, it's best to store the access token along with the time when the access token expires. When making an API call, first check to see if the current time is greater than the expiration time. If so, refresh the access token first, instead of waiting for the API server to reject your request because of an invalid access token. This will result in reduced latency because of fewer HTTP requests being made when the token expires.

Refreshing the access token is accomplished by making a HTTP POST to the token endpoint, specifying the grant_type as refresh_token and including the refresh_token. The request must also be authenticated.

Here's an example in PHP:

```php
<?php
include 'http_client.inc';

function getNewAccessToken($refreshToken) {
  $refreshTokenUrl = 'https://accounts.google.com/o/oauth2/token';

  // For example only.  Valid values for client_id and client_secret
  // need to be obtained for your environment from the Google APIs
  // Console at http://code.google.com/apis/console.
  $refreshTokenParams = array(
    'client_id' => '240195362.apps.googleusercontent.com',
    'client_secret' => 'hBMLD98Zi4wiqmiwmqDq',
    'grant_type' => 'refresh_token',
    'refresh_token' => $refreshToken
  );

  $httpClient = new HttpClient();
  $responseJson = $httpClient->postData(
      $refreshTokenUrl,
      $refreshTokenParams);
  $responseArray = json_decode($responseJson, TRUE);
  return $responseArray;
}

$responseArray = getNewAccessToken('adbadsfa12345');
$accessToken = $responseArray['access_token'];
$refreshToken = $responseArray['refresh_token'];
```

```
$expiresIn = $responseArray['expires_in'];
?>
```

This example authenticates the request by including the `client_id` and `client_secret` as HTTP POST parameters. Some OAuth providers may also support authenticating the request using the HTTP Basic access authentication method described in Step 2.

When requesting a new access token, a new refresh token may be issued as well. In this case, store the new refresh token and discard the previous one.

Step 4b: Obtaining a new access token

Regardless of whether API calls are being made direct from a user's browser or server-to-server, some applications only need access to a user's data while the user is "at the keyboard." In this case, the application may be able to request "online" access that results in no refresh token being issued and the access token having a limited lifespan. In this case, obtaining a new access token is done by sending the user through the authorization flow, starting at Step 1 again. Some API providers will not reprompt the user for access if the application has previously been granted access to the same set of data by the user and will instead redirect immediately back to the application with an authorization code.

Here are some specific implementations:

- **Google** defaults to "online" access and does not hand out refresh tokens unless explicitly requested by passing `access_type=offline` to the authorization endpoint at the time an authorization code is requested (see Step 1). In this case, the user is warned that they are granting permission for the application to "Perform these operations when I'm not using the application." If an application with only "online" access needs a new authorization code, it is automatically issued to the client without user interaction, and then exchanged by the application in a server-to-server call (see Step 2).

- **Facebook** defaults to "online" access: it issues access tokens with limited lifespan and does not issue refresh tokens. If an application needs offline access, it can request `offline_access` by specifying this permission as one of the values in the `scope` string. This will result in an access token being issued with an infinite expiration time, though the token will still be subject to potential revocation by the user.

How Can Access Be Revoked?

Different authorization servers have different policies as to when access tokens are revoked. Most typically enable the user to explicitly revoke access through an *account management* interface, though these interfaces can be difficult for users to find.

Additionally, some API providers (such as Facebook) revoke outstanding access tokens when a user changes their password.

Applications are not usually informed when a user revokes access, and the specification does not define any way to implement a notification—the app will simply see an error the next time it attempts to use an access token or refresh the token stored for that user.

Facebook, however, does have a definable "Deauthorize callback URL" which performs a HTTP POST to your application when a user revokes access in the style of a Web-Hook. More information is available in Facebook's developer documentation (*http://developers.facebook.com/docs/authentication*).

While users can revoke their access manually, some OAuth 2.0 authorization servers also allow tokens to be revoked programmatically. This enables an application to clean up after itself and remove access it no longer needs if, for instance, the user uninstalls the app.

Programmatic revocation is defined in a draft extension to the OAuth 2.0 specification (*http://tools.ietf.org/html/draft-lodderstedt-oauth-revocation*) and is implemented by popular OAuth providers such as Salesforce and Google. Salesforce allows for revocation of both refresh tokens and access tokens, while Google only enables revocation of refresh tokens. Here's an example revocation request:

```
curl "https://accounts.google.com/o/oauth2/revoke?token=ya29.AHES6ZSzF"
```

The extension also defines a JSONP "callback" query parameter that OAuth providers can optionally support. Both Salesforce and Google support this parameter.

A 200 response code indicates successful revocation.

CHAPTER 3

Client-Side Web Applications Flow

The Implicit Grant flow for browser-based client-side web applications is very simple. In this flow, an access token is immediately returned to the application after a user grants the requested authorization. An intermediate authorization code is not required as it is in the server-side Web Application flow (see Chapter 2).

Figure 3-1 shows a step-by-step flow diagram, based on a diagram from the specification.

When Should the Implicit Grant Flow Be Used?

The Implicit Grant flow should be used when

- Only temporary access to data is required.
- The user is regularly logged into the API provider.
- The OAuth client is running in the browser (using JavaScript, Flash, etc.).
- The browser is strongly trusted and there is limited concern that the access token will leak to untrusted users or applications.

Limitations of the Implicit Grant Flow

The Implicit Grant flow does not accommodate refresh tokens. If the Authorization server expires access tokens regularly, your application will need to run through the authorization flow whenever it needs access.

Some API providers, such as Google, will not reprompt the user for access if the user remains logged in and has approved the required scopes previously. The application can do this "refresh" process in the background as an iframe without any impact on the user experience.

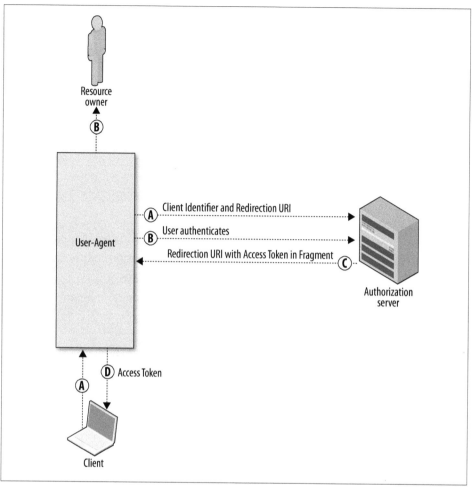

Figure 3-1. Client-Side Web Applications flow: Step-by-step

Security Properties

In the Implicit Grant flow, the application does not store long-lived refresh tokens on a server, limiting the exposure if the server is compromised. It also requires that the user be authenticated to the API provider's authorization server in order to "refresh" access tokens on the client, ensuring that a leaked access token's value is time-limited, depending on the OAuth implementation.

Because the access token is sent to the user's web browser, this flow offers less accountability than the Authorization Code flow. API calls that appear to have originated from a third-party app may have in fact been made directly by the resource owner themselves.

User Experience

A JavaScript-based Contacts picker for selecting users to invite to a Photo Viewer application is a great example use case for the Implicit Grant flow. It is a valuable activity for both the user and the application developer, it doesn't happen regularly, and the user is always responsible for choosing which users to invite from his or her contacts.

The user experience is identical to the Server-Side Web Application flow described in Chapter 2:

1. Photo Viewer application lets the user know that it needs access to her Contacts.
2. The OAuth authorization server used by the Contact app's API prompts the user to grant permission for the Photo Viewer application to read her contacts.
3. After the user has approved, she is redirected back to the Photo Viewer application, which now has access to her contacts.

Step-by-Step

Like in the case of the flow for Server-side Web Applications described in Chapter 2, you'll first need to register your application with the API provider (see "Developer and Application Registration" on page 8).

After registration is complete, it's time to write some code! We'll use simple HTML and JavaScript for this example.

Step 1: Let the user know what you're doing and request authorization

This step is very similar to the Authorization Code flow. Since requesting data access requires redirecting your users to the authorization server, it's a best practice to let them know in advance what will happen. You can do this by displaying a message, along with a link that directs the user to the OAuth authorization endpoint.

You can find the URL for the OAuth authorization endpoint in the API provider's documentation. For Google Tasks (and all other Google APIs using OAuth 2.0), the authorization endpoint is at

```
https://accounts.google.com/o/oauth2/auth
```

You will need to specify a few query parameters with this link:

client_id
: The value provided to you when you registered your application.

redirect_uri
: The location the user should be returned to after they approve access for your app. For this example, the application will use `https://photoviewer.saasyapp.com/oauth_response.html`.

scope

> The data your application is requesting access to. This is specified as a list of space-delimited strings. Valid values for the scope should be included in the API provider documentation. For Google Contacts, the scope is `https://www.google.com/m8/feeds/`.

response_type

> The `token` for the client-side Web Application flow, indicating that an access token will be returned to the application after the user approves the authorization request.

The complete code for handling this flow (in `index.html`) is long, so let's explore it in snippets.

This initial snippet opens a pop up window to the authorization URL. The `client_id`, scope, and `response_type` are set to the appropriate values. A pseudo-random state value is generated in order to mitigate the risk of CSRF attacks. We've also set the `redirect_uri` to a page that contains JavaScript for parsing the access token from the URL and passing it back to the parent window:

```
<script type="text/javascript">
  var clientId = '1032068783357.apps.googleusercontent.com';
  var authorizationUrlBase = 'https://accounts.google.com/o/oauth2/auth';
  var redirectUri = 'http://photoviewer.saasyapp.com/pv/oauth2callback.html';
  var scope = 'https://www.google.com/m8/feeds/';
  var state;

  function startOauth() {
    // generate a pseudo-random number for state
    var rand = Math.random();
    var dateTime = new Date().getTime();
    state = rand * dateTime;
    var url = authorizationUrlBase;
    url += '?response_type=token'
        + '&redirect_uri=' + encodeURIComponent(redirectUri)
        + '&client_id=' + encodeURIComponent(clientId)
        + '&scope=' + encodeURIComponent(scope)
        + '&state=' + encodeURIComponent(state);
    var w = window.open(url, '_blank', 'width=500,height=400');
  }
</script>
```

Error handling

See the description for error handling in Step 1 of the Server-side Web Applications flow (Chapter 2). The same error handling process applies to this flow.

Step 2: Parsing the access token from the URL

After the user approves access, the pop up window is redirected back to the specified `redirect_uri` and an `access_token` is included in the # hash fragment. Here's an example URL for this application:

```
http://photoviewer.saasyapp.com/pv/
oauth2callback.html#access_token=ya29.AHES6ZSzX&token_type=Bearer&expires_in=3600
```

JavaScript doesn't traditionally treat elements of the hash fragment as name/value pairs, so we need to parse out the value of the `access_token` and other elements of the OAuth response:

```
var oauthParams = {};

// parse the query string
// from http://oauthssodemo.appspot.com/step/2
var params = {}, queryString = location.hash.substring(1),
    regex = /([^&=]+)=([^&]*)/g, m;
while (m = regex.exec(queryString)) {
  oauthParams[decodeURIComponent(m[1])] = decodeURIComponent(m[2]);
}

...
```

Next, we need to pass the access token to the parent window:

```
window.opener.setOauthParams(oauthParams);
```

This passes the access token back to the main browser window. To protect against CSRF attacks, the `setOAuthParams` method should check that `oauthParams['state']` matches the global state variable set in `startOAuth` above.

This mechanism of communicating with the parent window works in modern browsers. However, the same-origin policy is enforced, so the pop up window needs to match the host/port/protocol of the main window.

Google has implemented a more elegant way for OAuth 2.0 pop up windows to communicate using the HTML5 `window.postMessage` feature. This is not widely deployed yet, but you can see a sample implementation on Google Project Hosting (*http://code .google.com/p/oauth2-postmessage-profile/*).

Step 3: Call the API

We use jQuery (*http://jquery.com/*) for calling the API to make it a bit easier. Instead, you could create a `<script>` element pointing to the JSONP URL for the Contacts API and dynamically append it to the `<head>` element of your webpage.

The `callApi()` function below will retrieve the user's contacts as JSON and call the setResponse function with the data:

```
function callApi() {
  var contactsUrl = 'https://www.google.com/m8/feeds/contacts/default/full?
v=3.0&alt=json-in-script';
  document.getElementById('access_request').style.display = 'none';
  var oauthParams = this.getOAuthParams();
  contactsUrl += "&access_token=" + encodeURIComponent(oauthParams['access_token']);
  $.ajax({
    'url': contactsUrl,
```

```
        'dataType': 'jsonp',
        'success': function(data) {
            setResponse(data);
        }
    });
}
```

Notice that we appended the `access_token` to the URL instead of using the preferred `Authorization` header mechanism. This is because jQuery does not allow manually setting the `Authorization` header used on these requests.

Step 4: Refreshing the access token

Unlike with the Authorization Code flow for server-side web applications, there is no special protocol for refreshing tokens when using the Implicit Grant flow. Your application will simply need to request a new access token using the same process as you used to fetch the initial token (Steps 1 to 3 above).

Some providers, like Google, will not present an authorization request to the user if they have previously approved access for your application. However, the user will need to be logged into their Google account for a new token to be issued without the authorization server prompting the user for their Google account password.

Although not standardized yet, support for an "immediate" mode also exists in some OAuth 2.0 providers. This allows this refresh process to occur in a hidden iframe, enabling a new access token to be transparently sent back to the application without the risk of prompting the user. If the user would otherwise be prompted to authenticate or grant access, immediate mode will instead cause the window to be redirected back to the app with an error message indicating the failure. This allows the app to gracefully prompt the user as needed for renewed authorization.

For the Google and Salesforce OAuth authorization endpoints, you can provide an additional query parameter value `immediate=true` to enable immediate mode.

How Can Access Be Revoked?

See the description for token revocation in the Server-side Web Applications flow (Chapter 2) section. The same token revocation process applies to this flow.

CHAPTER 4

Resource Owner Password Flow

The Resource Owner Password Credentials flow allows exchanging the username and password of a user for an access token and, optionally, a refresh token. This flow has significantly different security properties than the other OAuth flows. The primary difference is that the user's password is accessible to the application. This requires strong trust of the application by the user.

Figure 4-1 shows a step-by-step flow diagram, based on a diagram from the specification.

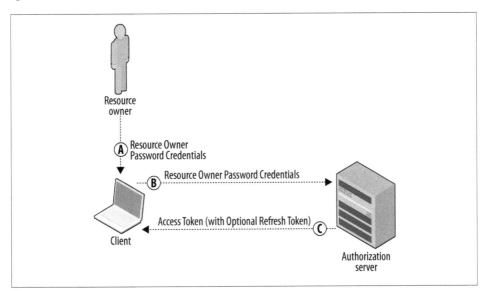

Figure 4-1. Resource Owner Password flow: Step-by-step

When Should the Resource Owner Password Flow Be Used?

Because the resource owner's password is exposed to the application, this flow should be used sparingly. It is recommended only for first-party "official" applications released by the API provider, and not opened up to wider third-party developer communities.

If a user is asked to type their password into "official" applications, they may become accustomed to doing so and become vulnerable to phishing attempts by other apps. In order to mitigate this concern, developers and IT administrators should clearly educate their users how they should determine which apps are "official" and which are not.

Security Properties

Although the application has access to the resource owner's password, there are still some security benefits to using this flow versus authenticating API calls with a username and password (via HTTP Basic access authentication or similar). With Basic authentication, an application needs to have continuous access to the user's password in order to make API calls. It also requires the user change their password and reenter the new password in all applications which require it, should the user no longer want an application to have access to their data.

However, if the OAuth Resource Owner Password flow is used, the application only needs access to the user's credentials once: on first use when the credentials are exchanged for an access token. This means there's no requirement for the app to store these credentials within the application or on the device, and revoking access is easy as well.

User Experience

The user experience for this flow is identical to typical password-based access requests. The application asks the user for their username and password and the user provides the information. The application then makes either a server-side or client-side request to the API provider's authorization server, without any user-facing interface changes.

If the API provider does not issue a `refresh_token` and the issued `access_token` is short-lived, the application will likely store the username and password for future authentication attempts. Unfortunately, this defeats some of the benefit of this flow.

Step-by-Step

To demonstrate this flow, we'll use an example built on top of Salesforce's REST-based APIs. Our example will retrieve and output all contacts accessible to the resource owner in the Salesforce CRM system.

We'll assume the example application is a native mobile application written by Acme Corporation and distributed to its employees through a corporate application directory. This method of distribution indicates to the employees that it is a "trusted" application and it's OK to enter their credentials in the app.

Step 1: Ask the user for their credentials

The first step is asking the user to provide their credentials to the application. In addition to a username and password, Salesforce requires that a user enter their *security token* when logging into an app from an untrusted network, such as the networks used by popular mobile phone service providers. An application would typically display this as a third field for user input, in addition to the username and password.

Step 2: Exchange the credentials for an access token

The process of exchanging credentials for an access token is very similar to exchanging an authorization code for an access token in the Authorization Code flow. We simply need to make a HTTP POST to the authorization server, providing the credentials and client information.

You can find the authorization server URL in the API provider's documentation. For Salesforce, the URL is

```
https://login.salesforce.com/services/oauth2/token
```

Here are the required POST parameters:

grant_type
: Specified as "password" for this flow.

scope
: The data your application is requesting access to. It is not required for Salesforce and is optional for other APIs. The Winter '12 version of Salesforce introduces optional values for this parameter.

client_id
: The value provided to you when you registered your application. Although optional in the spec, this value is required by Salesforce. Registration of the app is achieved using the App Setup→Develop→Remote Access menu.

client_secret
: The value provided to you when you registered your application. While the name of this parameter implies that the value is *secret*, it is sometimes required by API providers for nonconfidential clients such as native mobile applications. In these cases, the value is not actually a *secret*, as it could be discovered by users of the application.

username
: The username provided by the resource owner, encoded as UTF-8.

password

The password provided by the resource owner, encoded as UTF-8. For Salesforce, you need to concatenate the security token entered by the user at the end of the entered password and pass the combined value as the value of this parameter.

Here's an example request via the `curl` command-line HTTP client:

```
curl -d "grant_type=password" \
-d "client_id=3MVG9QDx8IKCsXTFMOo9aE3KfEwsZLvRt" \
-d "client_secret=4826278391389087694" \
-d "username=ryan%40ryguy.com" \
-d "password=_userspassword__userssecuritytoken_" \
https://login.salesforce.com/services/oauth2/token
```

If the user-provided credentials are successfully authenticated, the Salesforce OAuth authorization server will return an `application/json` response containing an `access_token`:

```
{
  "id":"https://login.salesforce.com/id/00DU0000000Io8rMAC/005U0000000hMDCIA2",
  "issued_at":"1316990706988",
  "instance_url":"https://na12.salesforce.com",
  "signature":"Q2KTt8Ez5dwJ4Adu6QttAhCxbEP3HyfaTUXoNI=",
  "access_token":"00DU0000000Io8r!AQcKbNiJPtOOCSAvxU2SBjVGP6hWOmfmKHO7QiPEGIX"
}
```

What do each of these response parameters mean?

access_token

The access token used to access the API on behalf of the user who provided their credentials. This is the only required item in the response.

id (*Salesforce-specific value*)

The unique identity of the user. This URL can also be accessed as any other OAuth-protected resource to obtain more information about the user. The user metadata is returned as JSON or XML, depending on the value of the HTTP `Accept` header sent in the request.

instance_url

The URL prefix the client application should use to access the API. This response parameter is specific to Salesforce's implementation.

signature

A signature used to validate that the identity URL hasn't been modified since being sent from the server. Although Salesforce issues signatures that can be verified, it isn't strictly necessary; instead, the application can use the built-in protections of HTTPS to ensure communication with Salesforce's servers. This response parameter is specific to Salesforce's implementation.

issued_at (*Salesforce-specific value*)

The time the signature was generated, used for validating it.

Step 3: Call the API

Since the OAuth access token issued by the authorization flow is a simple bearer token like the access tokens provided in the other flows (as described in "Step 3: Call the API" on page 24), it can be used similarly. You simply need to provide the access token via a HTTP `Authorization` header or query parameter value, depending on which the API provider supports.

Here's an example `curl` request:

```
curl -d "q=SELECT+name+FROM+Account"\
-H 'Authorization: Bearer 00DU0000000Io8r!AQcAQKJ.Cg1dCBCVHmx2.Iu3lroPQBV2P65_jXk'
"https://na12.salesforce.com/services/data/v20query"
```

Step 4: Refresh the access token

Although Salesforce does not support refreshing the access token when using this flow, the spec does accommodate it using the method described in "Step 4a: Refresh the access token" on page 26.

It is important that clients have a way of refreshing the access token if it is issued with only a short-term lifespan. This prevents developers from needing to store the provided user credentials within their applications—one of the major benefits of this flow versus traditional HTTP Basic access authentication mechanisms.

CHAPTER 5

Client Credentials Flow

Most of the OAuth flows are for handling delegated authorization, when a resource owner grants access to an application to access her data. However, there are cases when the client itself owns the data and does not need delegated access from a resource owner, or delegated access has already been granted to the application outside of a typical OAuth flow.

This flow (shown in Figure 5-1) works well for similar use cases as the "2-legged" flow in OAuth 1.0.

Figure 5-1. Client Credentials flow: Step-by-step

When Should the Client Credentials Flow Be Used?

Imagine a storage API, such as Google Storage or Amazon S3. You're building an application that has resources (data files, images, etc.) stored externally to your app using one of these APIs. The application needs to read and update these resources, but acting on behalf of the app itself rather than on behalf of any individual user. This is a perfect use case for the Client Credentials flow. The application can ask the OAuth authorization server for an access token directly, without the involvement of any end user.

There is another representative case for the Client Credentials flow—when a resource owner has granted an application access to their resources out of band, without using a typical OAuth flow. Google provides a concrete use case in the Google Apps

Marketplace. When an application is listed on the Marketplace, vendors get credentials that represent their application and also register the scopes of data they need access to. When the application is later installed by an organization's IT administrator, Google asks the administrator whether it's OK to grant the application access to his organization's data. When access is approved, Google stores that organization "Acme Corp" has granted access to "Google Calendar and Google Contacts" for application "Task Manager Pro." Google does not issue any tokens to the application. When the application tries to access data in the future, Google simply looks up whether the application is allowed access to data for the particular organization.

What APIs Support the Client Credentials Flow?

While the preceding paragraphs describe some potential use cases for this flow, these providers (Google and Amazon) have not yet implemented the Client Credentials flow in OAuth 2.0. However, Facebook has implemented this flow for its applications, to be able to perform App Login. App Login is required for certain Facebook API calls, including the ability to get app statistics and user demographics from the App Insights service.

How Does the Client Authenticate?

This flow is reliant upon the client being able to properly authenticate with the authorization server and the client's authentication credentials remaining confidential. In order to authenticate, the client can pass the `client_id` and `client_secret` to the authorization server as `POST` parameters in the access token request or can use a HTTP Basic `Authentication` header. The authorization server can also authenticate the client using other mechanisms, such as a public/private key pair, SSL/TLS client authentication, and the like.

Security Properties

Depending on the precise use case the Client Credentials flow is used for, a single set of credentials for a client could provide access to a large amount of data. The more data a single set of credentials has access to, the greater the risk if the credentials become compromised. It is extremely critical that the credentials used to authenticate the client be kept highly confidential. Ideally, these credentials would also be regularly rotated.

Step-by-Step

To demonstrate this flow, we'll use Facebook's implementation of App Login with the App Insights service.

Step 1: Exchange the application's credentials for an access token

The application needs to request an access token from the authorization server, authenticating the request with its client credentials.

You can find the authorization server's token URL in the API provider's documentation. For Facebook, the URL is

```
https://graph.facebook.com/oauth/access_token
```

Here are the required POST parameters:

grant_type
> Specified as "client_credentials" for this flow.

client_id
> The value provided to you when you registered your application.

client_secret
> The value provided to you when you registered your application.

Here's an example request via the curl command-line HTTP client:

```
curl -d "grant_type=client_credentials\
&client_id=2016271111111117128396\
&client_secret=904b98aaaaaaac1c92381d2" \
https://graph.facebook.com/oauth/access_token
```

If the client credentials are successfully authenticated, an access token is returned to the client. As Facebook has implemented an earlier version of the OAuth 2.0 specification as of the time of this writing, it returns the access_token in the body of the response using form url-encoding:

```
access_token=2016271111111117128396|8VGOriNauEzttXkUXBtUbw
```

The latest draft of the spec (v22) states that the authorization server should instead return an application/json response containing the access_token:

```
{
    "access_token":"2016271111111117128396|8VGOriNauEzttXkUXBtUbw"
}
```

The access token is then used to access the API on behalf of the application itself.

Step 2: Call the API

Since the OAuth access token issued by the Client Credentials flow is a bearer token like the access tokens provided in the other flows, it can be used similarly. You simply need to provide the access token via a HTTP Authorization header or query parameter value, depending on which the API provider supports.

Here's an example curl request, using a query parameter to pass the access token:

```
curl "https://graph.facebook.com/202627763128396/insights?\
access_token=2016271111111117128396|8VGOriNauEzttXkUXBtUbw"
```

Facebook supports passing the access token as a HTTP `Authorization` header as well, but using the older `Authorization: OAuth tokenvalue` instead of `Authorization: Bearer tokenvalue`.

When the Access Token Expires

The Client Credentials flow typically provides a long-lived access token. The authorization server may indicate an `expires_in` time; however, the protocol does not support issuing a refresh token in response to the Client Credentials flow. Instead, the application simply asks for a new access token if the current one expires.

CHAPTER 6

Getting Access to User Data from Mobile Apps

There are two main classes of mobile applications: mobile-optimized web apps using HTML5 and other web technologies and native mobile applications. While mobile-optimized web apps can use the traditional OAuth client-side or Web Application flows with some special consideration for user experience, native mobile applications require additional considerations.

Why You Should Use OAuth for Native Mobile Apps

When building a native mobile app, there are two primary reasons you should consider using OAuth:

Access to your own APIs
Many mobile applications have backend servers that they use to keep track of user data. Perhaps your app is a game and stores high scores and level completion data in a server-side database to enable social functionality or supporting playing the game on multiple platforms. In this case, your app needs to communicate with the backend using an API, typically a REST-based HTTP API. OAuth is a great way to handle API authorization for these types of applications, and it enables you to build and maintain only one interface for users to log in to your application, whether they're on the Web or using your native mobile companion app.

Access to APIs from other providers
Some API providers may require you to use OAuth for API authorization. However, for those that don't, there are still several great reasons you want to use OAuth for native mobile apps: you have an obligation to help users stay safe and also a desire to make your application easy to use by all users. Asking users for their password for third-party services reinforces this pattern and makes users more vulnerable to phishing attempts. This further requires that your app have access to the user's entire account (as opposed to a limited scope of data) and requires your app to

store the user's credentials on the device for long-lived access, potentially leaving them open to compromise. Another primary reason that you want to consider using OAuth is that some users at specific API providers may simply not be able to delegate access to your app with a typical username and password because they use a second-factor authentication scheme (such as a one-time password key token) or their account is federated to another identity provider (via OpenID, SAML, etc.).

What Flow Should Be Used for Native Mobile Apps?

The available flows for native mobile apps will likely be restricted based on what flows are supported by your API provider. However, there are a few questions you can consider when deciding what flow to use.

Do You Have a Mobile Backend Web Server for Your Application?

Yes: If you have a mobile backend web server for your native app, you can use one of the typical OAuth flows for web applications: the client-side (implicit) flow or the flow for server-side web apps. The same considerations apply: Do you need long-lived "offline" access from your mobile app's backend server? Use the server-side web app flow. Or do you need short-lived one-time access directly from the native app? Use the client-side implicit flow.

When using the server-side web app flow and passing an authorization code to your server, the user of the app will still need to be authenticated to the app backend, similar to how a user is authenticated to web application servers using session cookies.

No: If your application does not have a mobile backend web server powering it, you need to use some type of native application flow. This can be very similar to the server-side web app flow or the client-side implicit flow, but there are two restrictions: you don't have a web server to use for the `redirect_uri`, and you should maintain the confidentiality of any `client_secret` values, which are sometimes required for the server-side flow.

Depending on the mobile platform you're building on and the API provider you're using, you can use a custom URI scheme such as *my-mobile-app://oauth/callback* for the `redirect_uri` in order to return the authorization code or `access_token` to your application. However, on some platforms, these custom URI schemes can be registered by multiple applications (and their uniqueness is not guaranteed), so there is a risk that the tokens could be intercepted by the wrong app on the device and used maliciously. It's also possible that your API provider requires preregistration of these `redirect_uri` values and does not accept values using custom URI schemes.

There are also some API providers supporting a *native client flow*. With the native client flow, a special `redirect_uri` value is used to send the authorization code or access token to a web page hosted by the OAuth authorization server. The user can then copy/paste this value into the application or the application can programmatically grab the value from the body or window title and close the web browser window.

The currently proposed special `redirect_uri` value for the native client flow is `urn:ietf:wg:oauth:2.0:oob`. Figure 6-1 shows an example result web page after the user approves access to their data. In most cases, the user would never see this page, however, because the application would grab the access token and close the window before it is visible.

Figure 6-1. Google's response page when using the OOB redirect_uri for native clients

The (Ugly) Web Browser

Many mobile application developers have objected to using OAuth for their native applications because it requires either embedding a WebView or opening up the system web browser on the device. They don't view either of these as good options, as a web browser often *feels different* than a native UI.

This is a reasonable concern, though we always need to balance security and usability. We should expect that the user experience for these OAuth browser-based flows will continue to improve along with increased pervasiveness of HTML5 technology and mobile web UX design techniques.

Embedded WebView

The embedded WebView has become a popular way to handle OAuth authorization grants for native mobile applications. Instead of opening up the system web browser (via an `Intent` on Android or `UIApplication` on iOS), the embedded WebView simply includes a browser within the main application window. This mechanism leads to a smaller context switch for the user, while at the same time providing the native app greater control over the web browser.

Primary advantage

- WebViews are easily controlled by the native application. This enables the application to easily access the OAuth access token or authorization code by examining the cookie store or the title of the application window, without worrying about the issues of registering a custom URL scheme.

Some disadvantages

- WebViews don't display the trust indicators present in the system web browser (such as the SSL/TLS lock indicating certificate chain validation and the URL of the site). Users may be prompted to enter their credentials to log in to the OAuth authorization provider. This results in users being more vulnerable to phishing attacks if evil apps are deployed onto user devices.
- With separate cookie and history stores, the user is not logged into any accounts. This means that they must login to the OAuth Authorization Server before granting access to an app, and entering credentials on mobile devices can sometimes be a painful experience.

System Web Browser

Opening up the system web browser seems like the natural way to send a user through an OAuth grant flow, but as with the embedded WebView, there are both advantages and disadvantages to this technique.

Some advantages

- The system web browser uses the system cookie store. If your application integrates with a popular API provider, it's likely that the user is already logged into the provider—resulting in a simple single-click grant process. Users don't need to re-type their password.
- Users have greater security assurances with the system web browser, as they're accustomed to the typical security indicators (such as the SSL/TLS lock and the URL of the site). This makes users less vulnerable to phishing.

Some disadvantages

- Using the system web browser requires that the user be returned to the native app after granting access. As mentioned above, this typically done using a custom URI scheme such as *my-mobile-app://oauth/callback* for the `redirect_uri`. Because there is no central registry of these custom schemes, other malicious applications installed on the device may be able to intercept the OAuth access tokens or authorization codes.

- The history store of the system web browser cannot be controlled by the native app, leading to potential compromise of OAuth access tokens if the implicit flow is used. While this is also a problem on desktop web browsers, it's more of a concern with mobile devices, which are more portable and thus more susceptible to loss and theft. This risk is usually mitigated by the short validity of OAuth access tokens.

Enhanced Mobile App Authorization for Specific Providers

Some OAuth providers have built special mobile libraries or applications to make doing OAuth easier on devices and to improve the user experience.

For Google

On its Android operating system, Google provides a service called the AccountManager (*http://developer.android.com/reference/android/accounts/AccountManager.html*). Originally this service was designed to allow applications to request auth tokens for Google APIs using the proprietary ClientLogin mechanism. However, this service has been updated to support getting OAuth 2.0 access tokens for Google APIs.

In order to get an OAuth 2.0 access token, you simply need to call `AccountMan ager.getAuthToken()` to request a token using an `authTokenType` of `oauth2:<scope>`. For example, to request access to the Google Tasks API, specify an `authTokenType` of `oauth2:https://www.googleapis.com/auth/tasks`. Unfortunately, this literal string will be presented to users when they're asked to grant access, so using this technique is not recommended. However, for some APIs, such as Google Tasks, there are aliases such as Manage Your Tasks that can be used in place of the `oauth2:<scope>` value to produce a much friendlier request.

After you call `getAuthToken()`, the account manager will ask the user to approve or deny the request using a native application prompt. If the user approves the request, the application will be issued an `access_token` value, which can be used in API requests.

The Google Tasks API team has created an article (*http://code.google.com/apis/tasks/articles/oauth-and-tasks-on-android.html*) with more details on using this technique. Although other Google APIs may not have user-friendly aliases such as Manage Your Tasks, the general techniques described in the article will still apply.

Google does not have similar functionality available for iOS at the time of this writing. However, Google does have a client library for Objective-C (*http://code.google.com/p/gtm-oauth2/wiki/Introduction*) which makes creating an embedded WebView OAuth flow very easy to implement on iOS.

For Facebook

Facebook has SDKs available for both Android (*http://developers.facebook.com/docs/reference/androidsdk/*) and iOS (*http://developers.facebook.com/docs/reference/iossdk/*) that automatically prompt the user for requested permissions.

On Android, you call `Facebook.authorize()` and wait for the user to approve the authorization request. After the user approves, you can call `Facebook.getAccessToken()` to get an access token for use with the requested APIs.

CHAPTER 7

OpenID Connect Authentication

Nearly every web application prompts users to create an account and log in. In order to create an account, users are asked to provide their name, their email address, a password, and password confirmation. Not only does this take a lot of effort for the user (50+ keystrokes), but it also creates security concerns, as users often create the same password on multiple sites and some sites do not properly secure these credentials.

OpenID exists to enable federated identity, where users are able to authenticate with the same identity across multiple web applications. Both users and web applications trust identity providers, such as Google, Yahoo!, and Facebook, to store user profile information and authenticate users on behalf of the application. This eliminates the need for each web application to build its own custom authentication system, and it makes it much easier and faster for users to sign up and sign into sites around the Web.

OpenID Connect is the next-generation version of OpenID. The development of OpenID Connect has taken into account two key concepts:

- Passing permission to access authentication information (the user's identity) to a site is very similar to passing along delegated access to a user's data (such as their calendar). Developers shouldn't have to use entirely different protocols for these two different use cases—especially because many developers need to handle both in their applications.

- The specification should be modular—enabling spec compliance without requiring implementation of automated discovery, associations, and other complex bits included in the previous versions of OpenID.

The basic flow for OpenID Connect is:

1. The application requests OAuth 2.0 authorization for one or more of the OpenID Connect scopes (`openid`, `profile`, `email`, `address`) by redirecting the user to an identity provider.

2. After the user approves the OAuth authorization request, the user's web browser is redirected back to the application using a traditional OAuth flow. The app makes

a request to the Check ID Endpoint. This endpoint returns the user's identity (`user_id`) as well as other bits, such as the `aud` and `state`, which must be verified by the client to ensure valid authentication.

3. If the client requires additional profile information about the user, such as the user's full name, picture, and email address, the client can make requests to the UserInfo Endpoint.

Because OpenID Connect is built on top of OAuth 2.0 and is designed as a modular specification, it's much easier for you to implement federated authentication for your website in a compliant way. Since this is a Getting Started book, this chapter will primarily discuss the OpenID Connect Basic Client (*http://openid.net/specs/openid-connect -basic-1_0.html*) implementation.

ID Token

With OpenID Connect authentication, there is an additional type of OAuth token: an ID token. The ID token, or `id_token`, represents the identity of the user being authenticated. This is a separate token from the access token, which is used to retrieve the user's profile information or other user data requested during the same authorization flow.

The ID token is a JSON Web Token (JWT), which is a digitally signed and/or encrypted representation of the user's identity asserted by the identity provider. Instead of using cryptographic operations to validate the JSON Web Token, it can be treated as an opaque string and passed to the Check ID Endpoint for interpretation (see below). This flexibility keeps with the spirit of OAuth 2.0 and OpenID Connect being significantly easier to use than their predecessors.

Security Properties

Although the end user flow is quite similar, the security precautions necessary for authentication are much different than those for authorization because of the potential for replay attacks. Replay attacks occur when legitimate credentials are sent multiple times for malicious purposes.

There are two main types of replay attacks we wish to prevent:

* An attacker capturing a user's OAuth credentials as they log in to a site and using them later on the same site.

* A rogue application developer using the OAuth token a user was issued to log in to their malicious app in order to impersonate the user on a different legitimate app.

The OAuth 2.0 specification requires the OAuth endpoint and APIs to be accessed over SSL/TLS to prevent man-in-the-middle attacks, such as the first case.

Preventing rogue application developers from replaying legitimate OAuth credentials their app received in order to impersonate one of their users on another app requires a solution specific to OpenID Connect. This solution is the Check ID Endpoint. The Check ID Endpoint is used to verify that the credentials issued by the OAuth provider were issued to the correct application.

It is recommended that all developers use the Check ID Endpoint or decode the JSON Web Token to verify the asserted identity, though this is not strictly necessary in some cases when the application uses the server-side Web Application flow and the UserInfo Endpoint provides all required information.

The server-side Web Application flow, when implemented as per the specification, only issues an authorization code through the user's web browser. The web application should not ever accept an access token or identity token directly from the browser. The access token and identity token are retrieved by exchanging the authorization code in a server-to-server request. Since this exchange requires the server-to-server call to be authenticated with the client ID and client secret of the app which the authorization code was issued for, the OAuth token service will naturally prevent an app from accidentally using an authorization code issued to another app.

Alternatively, the client-side Web Application flow issues an access token and identity token directly to the app through the browser using a hash fragment. The access token and identity token are often sent to the backend web server using JavaScript in order to authenticate the user. In this case, the web server must either cryptographically verify the ID Token or call the Check ID endpoint to verify it was issued to the correct application. This is called "verifying the audience" of the token. See "Check ID Endpoint" on page 54 for more information.

Obtaining User Authorization

The process of obtaining user authorization for OpenID Connect is nearly identical to the process of obtaining authorization for any OAuth 2.0 enabled API. You can use either the client-side implicit flow (as described in Chapter 3) or the server-side web app flow (as described in Chapter 2).

As with any usage of these flows, the client generates a URL pointing at the OAuth Authorization Endpoint and redirects the user to that URL. The following parameters are passed:

client_id
> The value provided to you when you registered your application.

redirect_uri
> The location the user should be returned to after they approve the authentication request.

scope

> openid for a basic OpenID Connect request. If your client needs access to additional profile information for the user, additional scopes can be profiled in this space-delimited string: profile, email, address.

response_type

> id_token to indicate that an id_token is required for the application. Additionally, a response type of token or code must be included, separating the two response types by a space. token indicates the client-side Web Application flow, while code indicates the server-side Web Application flow.

nonce

> A unique value used by your application to protect against replay and cross-site request forgery (CSRF) attacks on your implementation. The value should be a random unique string for this particular request, unguessable and kept secret in the client (perhaps in a server-side session). This identical value will be included in the ID token response (see below).

The following is an example of a complete Authorization Endpoint URL, using the client-side implicit flow:

```
https://accounts.example.com/oauth2/auth?
  scope=openid+email&
  nonce=53f2495d7b435ac571&
  redirect_uri=https%3A%2F%2Foauth2demo.appspot.com%2Foauthcallback&
  response_type=id_token+token&
  client_id=753560681145-2ik2j3snsvbs80ijdi8.apps.googleusercontent.com
```

After the user approves the authentication request, they will be redirected back to the redirect_uri. Since this request uses the implicit flow, the redirect will include an access token that can be used with the UserInfo Endpoint to obtain profile information about the user. Additionally, and specific to OpenID Connect, the redirect will also include an id_token, which can be sent to the Check ID Endpoint to get the user's identity.

Here's an example redirect:

```
https://oauth2demo.appspot.com/oauthcallback#
  access_token=ya29.AHES6ZSzX
  token_type=Bearer&
  expires_in=3600&
  id_token=eyJhbGciOiJSUzI1NiJ9.eyJpc3MiOiJhY2NvdW50cy5nb29nbGUuY29tIiwiY...
```

The client then needs to parse the appropriate parameters from the hash fragment in the URL and call the Check ID Endpoint to validate the response.

Check ID Endpoint

The Check ID Endpoint exists to validate the id_token returned along with the OAuth 2.0 access_token by ensuring that it was intended for the correct client and is used by the client to begin an authenticated session. As described above, this check is required for the implicit flow for client-side applications (described in Chapter 3). If this check isn't done correctly, the client becomes vulnerable to replay attacks.

Here's an example Check ID endpoint request:

```
https://accounts.example.com/oauth2/tokeninfo?
  id_token=eyJhbGciOiJSUzI1NiJ9.eyJpc3MiOiJhY2NvdW50cy5nb29nbGUuY29tIiwiY...
```

And the response:

```
{
  "iss" : "https://accounts.example.com",
  "user_id" : "113487456102835830811",
  "aud" : "753560681145-2ik2j3snsvbs80ijdi8.apps.googleusercontent.com",
  "exp" : 1311281970
  "nonce" : 53f2495d7b435ac571
}
```

If the response is returned without a standard OAuth 2.0 error, the following checks need to be performed:

• Verify the `aud` value in the response is identical to the `client_id` used in the Authorization request.
• Verify that the `nonce` value in the response matches the value used in the Authorization request.

If this verification is completed successfully, the `user_id` is known to represent the unique identifier for the authenticated user, within the scope of the issuer (`iss`). If storing the identifier in a user database table and multiple identity providers are supported by your application, it is recommended that both values be stored upon account creation and queried upon each subsequent authentication request.

UserInfo Endpoint

While the Check ID Endpoint will return a unique identifier for the user authenticating to your application, many applications require additional information, such as the user's name, email address, profile photo, or birthdate. This profile information can be returned by the UserInfo Endpoint.

The UserInfo Endpoint is a standard OAuth-authorized REST API, with JSON responses. As when accessing any other API using OAuth, the `access_token` can be passed either as an `Authorization` header or as a URL query parameter.

Here's an example UserInfo request:

```
GET /v1/userinfo HTTP/1.1
Host: accounts.example.com
Authorization: Bearer ya29.AHES6ZSzX
```

With the response:

```
{
  "user_id": "3191142839810811",
  "name": "Example User",
  "given_name": "Example",
  "family_name": "User",
  "email": "user@example.com",
  "verified": true,
  "profile": "http://profiles.example.com/user",
  "picture": "https://photos.profiles.example.com/user/photo.jpg",
  "gender": "female",
  "birthday": "1982-02-11",
  "locale": "en-US"
}
```

OpenID Connect does not define any specific profile fields as required and does allow for additional profile fields to be included in the response.

Performance Improvements

The objective of the call to the Check ID Endpoint is to verify the legitimacy of the id_token. However, this requires an additional HTTP request to the OpenID Connect identity provider. This additional request can be avoided since the id_token is returned as a signed JSON Web Token (JWT) instead of as an opaque blob. The JWT includes the same information that is typically returned by the Check ID Endpoint, but the value is also cryptographically signed by the server in a way that can be validated by the client.

This gives the client the option to verify the signature using the JWT (for best performance) or simply call the Check ID Endpoint if the client wants to avoid cryptography.

Practical OpenID Connect

Since the OpenID Connect specification is still under active development, experimental implementations by identity providers still differ from the specification. Here are some example requests and responses using these experimental implementations.

For Google

Google's OpenID Connect implementation (see Figure 7-1) uses the following Endpoints:

Check ID
    https://www.googleapis.com/oauth2/v1/tokeninfo
UserInfo
    https://www.googleapis.com/oauth2/v1/userinfo

Google does not have the generic openid scope, but it supports the following main scopes for its OpenID Connect implementation:

Email
> https://www.googleapis.com/auth/userinfo.email

Profile
> https://www.googleapis.com/auth/userinfo.profile

Here's an example authorization URL for Google's OpenID Connect implementation:

```
https://accounts.google.com/o/oauth2/auth?
  scope=https%3A%2F%2Fwww.googleapis.com%2Fauth%2Fuserinfo.email+https%3A%2F
%2Fwww.googleapis.com%2Fauth%2Fuserinfo.profile&
  state=ABC123456&
  redirect_uri=https%3A%2F%2Foauthssodemo.appspot.com%2Foauthcallback&
  response_type=token%20id_token&
  client_id=8819981768.apps.googleusercontent.com
```

Figure 7-1. Google asking if it's OK to share info with example app "OAuth SSO Relying Party"

In this example, we're specifying a response_type of token id_token, indicating that we're looking for both an ID token and a traditional OAuth 2.0 access token (via the implicit flow). After the user approves the request by clicking "Allow Access," Google redirects back to the redirect_uri and includes an id_token and an access_token in the hash fragment of the URL. The id_token is a JSON Web Token (JWT) and contains the user's ID. This ID token can be validated by comparing a cryptographic signature or the Check ID Endpoint can be called. For simplicity, we'll show how to call the Check ID Endpoint. Here's an example request:

```
https://www.googleapis.com/oauth2/v1/tokeninfo?
  id_token=eyJhbGciOiJSUzI1NiJ9.eyJpc3MiOiJhY2NvdW50cy5nb29nbGUuY29tIiwiY...
```

Here's the response:

```
{
  "issued_to" : "8819981768.apps.googleusercontent.com",
```

```
    "user_id" : "113487456102835830811",
    "audience" : "8819981768.apps.googleusercontent.com",
    "expires_in" : 3465
}
```

After the Check ID response is properly validated by ensuring it's been issued for the correct application (by comparing the value of the issued_to parameter to the app's client ID), the app may wish to obtain additional profile information about the user. This information, such as the user's name or email address, can be obtained as a JSON response from the UserInfo Endpoint. The OAuth access_token must be sent to authorize the request. Here's an example request:

```
GET /oauth2/v1/userinfo HTTP/1.1
Host: www.googleapis.com
Authorization: Bearer ya29.AHES6ZSzX
```

Here's the response:

```
{
  "id": "110634877589748180443",
  "email": "ryan.boyd@gmail.com",
  "verified_email": true,
  "name": "Ryan Boyd",
  "given_name": "Ryan",
  "family_name": "Boyd",
  "link": "http://profiles.google.com/110634877589748180443",
  "picture": "https://lh6.googleusercontent.com/-XC1Cwt4OgfY/AAAAAAAAAAI/AAAAAAAACR8/
SU9W99JQFvc/photo.jpg",
  "gender": "male",
  "birthday": "0000-10-05",
  "locale": "en-US"
}
```

You'll notice that the response indicates my birth year as 0000. I'm not that old; Google uses this special value to indicate that the birth year is not shared.

For Facebook

Facebook's implementation of identity using OAuth 2.0 isn't documented as being OpenID Connect. However, it works similarly to the specification, with a few minor differences to account for in client code.

Facebook uses the following Endpoint:

UserInfo
  https://graph.facebook.com/me

Facebook does not provide Check ID Endpoint functionality, and for this reason I recommend using only the Authorization Code flow for server-side applications (described in Chapter 2) and not the implicit flow for client-side applications. If you use the client-side Web Application flow, you'll have no ability to verify the access token was intended for use by your application, and thus can leave your app vulnerable to replay attacks.

Here we can see an example authorization URL for Facebook's OpenID Connect implementation:

```
https://www.facebook.com/dialog/oauth?
    client_id=202627763128396&
    redirect_uri=https%3A%2F%2Foauth2demo.appspot.com%2Foauthcallback&
    state=ABC123456
```

Since a scope is not specified, Facebook defaults to requesting authorization for public profile information. Additional information can be requested by specifying scope values such as email, read_stream. Notice that Facebook uses comma-delimited scope values instead of space-delimited values as defined by the latest OAuth 2.0 specification.

Since a response_type is not specified, Facebook defaults to the Authorization Code flow for server-side web applications. If you wish to use the implicit flow for client-side web applications, specify a response_type=token, though this is not recommended.

As is typical with the Authorization Code flow for server-side web applications described in Chapter 2, the user's browser will be redirected to the application's redirect_uri after the user approves access. The redirect URL will include an authorization code in the code query parameter. The application then needs to exchange the authorization code for an access token by making a request to the Token Endpoint.

While the authorization code exchange typically uses a HTTP POST, Facebook also supports using a HTTP GET:

```
https://graph.facebook.com/oauth/access_token?
        client_id=202627763128396&
        redirect_uri=https%3A%2F%2Foauth2demo.appspot.com%2Foauthcallback&
        client_secret=YOUR_APP_SECRET&code=123456
```

Since we're using the Authorization Code flow for server-side web applications, there is no need to do a Check ID request. This is because the Authorization Code flow requires the application's credentials to be sent securely to the server when exchanging an authorization code for an access token, resulting in an automatic check that the authorization code was issued to the current client. However, the application must keep the access token confidential on the server and prevent trusting any access token directly sent by the user, or the application could be vulnerable to the same type of replay attack that the Check ID endpoint was designed to prevent.

At this point, the application can obtain profile information for the user via the me endpoint of the Graph API. Here's an example request:

```
https://graph.facebook.com/me?
    access_token=123456abc123456abc
```

Here's the response:

```
{
    "id":"545296355",
```

```
    "name":"Ryan Boyd",
    "first_name":"Ryan",
    "last_name":"Boyd",
    "link":"http:\/\/www.facebook.com\/rboyd",
    "username":"rboyd",
    "hometown":{
       "id":"114952118516947",
       "name":"San Francisco, California"
    },
    "location":{
       "id":"114952118516947",
       "name":"San Francisco, California"
    },
    "gender":"male",
    "email":"ryan\u0040ryguy.com",
    "timezone":-8,
    "locale":"en_US",
    "verified":true,
    "updated_time":"2011-06-03T18:37:40+0000"
}
```

OpenID Connect Evolution

The protocol is likely to change after receiving feedback from both identity providers and relying parties. Information on the current Developer Preview can be found on the OpenID Foundation site (*http://openid.net/connect/*), including the detailed specifications and mailing lists to follow development of the specifications.

CHAPTER 8

Tools and Libraries

Although OAuth 2.0 is relatively young, there are still a variety of tools and libraries available for developers to make using it easier.

Google's OAuth 2.0 Playground

Google has built a new version of its OAuth Playground tool for OAuth 2.0 (see Figure 8-1). The OAuth 2.0 Playground (*https://code.google.com/oauthplayground/*) demonstrates the three-step process for a typical server-side web application Authorization Code flow: getting an authorization code, exchanging it for an access token, and making API requests. It also supports the Implicit flow for client-side web applications.

While the default configuration is to use Google's APIs and OAuth endpoints, the tool does enable you to specify a custom client ID, client secret, and custom endpoints. Salesforce has blogged about (*http://blogs.developerforce.com/developer-relations/2011/11/calling-the-force-com-apis-from-google-oauth-2-0-playground.html*) how to use the tool with their APIs.

> This tool is made available by Google for educational and testing purposes. While it exposes the OAuth access token to the web browser (and resource owner), this should not normally be done when using the Authorization Code flow and confidential clients. Also, specifying custom client ID and client secret values requires those credentials be sent to the OAuth Playground server.

Google's TokenInfo Endpoint

Google's endpoint for the Check ID step of OpenID Connect can be used to validate any OAuth 2.0 token issued by Google. The endpoint at *https://www.googleapis.com/oauth2/v1/tokeninfo* is a simple read-only API. To get the scope and expiration date of

Figure 8-1. Google's OAuth Playground

a token, make a HTTP request to the endpoint and pass an OAuth access token as the `access_token` query parameter or an ID token as the `id_token` parameter.

Apigee's Console

The Apigee Console enables exploring APIs from 20+ API providers, such as Facebook, Twitter, Salesforce, and SoundCloud. For those APIs supporting OAuth, it performs a typical OAuth flow, though without exposing the protocol-level details of the OAuth exchange. After OAuth authorization is granted using a variety of versions of the OAuth 1.0 and OAuth 2.0 draft specifications, it provides easy access to call APIs by selecting prepopulated endpoint URLs. With each API request, the console displays the detailed HTTP request and response details.

Facebook's Access Token Tool and Access Token Debugger

Facebook provides an Access Token Tool (*https://developers.facebook.com/tools/access_token/*), which issues access tokens that can be used for testing and debugging. Both user-based and app-based tokens are issued. The user tokens issued by the tool are similar to those issued by the server-side Web Application flow or client-side flow. The app tokens issued by the tool are similar to those issued by the Client Credentials flow.

They also provide an Access Token Debugger (*https://developers.facebook.com/tools/debug*), which displays information about OAuth access tokens, including the scopes, validity, issue time, expiration time and more.

Libraries

Many major API providers build and maintain client libraries for accessing their specific services. Some of these libraries, such as the Google API Clients and Facebook SDKs provide built-in support for OAuth 2.0. When OAuth support is provided, these libraries often abstract the implementations enough to make it really easy to implement.

Here are some API-specific client libraries which implement OAuth 2.0:

- Google APIs Client Libraries for Java (*http://code.google.com/p/google-api-java-client/*), Objective-C (*http://code.google.com/p/google-api-objectivec-client/*), PHP (*http://code.google.com/p/google-api-php-client/*), Python (*http://code.google.com/p/google-api-python-client/*), Ruby (*http://code.google.com/p/google-api-ruby-client/*), JavaScript (*http://code.google.com/p/google-api-javascript-client/*)

- Facebook SDKs for JavaScript (*http://developers.facebook.com/docs/reference/javascript/*), Android (*http://developers.facebook.com/docs/reference/androidsdk*), iOS (*http://developers.facebook.com/docs/reference/iossdk*), PHP (*http://developers.facebook.com/docs/reference/php*)

- Foursquare does not provide official libraries, but it links to many community-contributed (*https://developer.foursquare.com/docs/libraries.html*) libraries, many of which support OAuth 2.0

Some of these libraries make it trivially easy to implement OAuth 2.0. Here's an example using Google's Python library on App Engine with the library's decorator pattern. This example requires only a few lines of OAuth-specific code:

```
from oauth2client.appengine import OAuth2Decorator
...
decorator = OAuth2Decorator(
    client_id='CLIENT_ID_FROM_DAILYMOTION',
    client_secret='CLIENT_SECRET_FROM_DAILYMOTION',
    scope='read',
    auth_uri='https://api.dailymotion.com/oauth/authorize',
    token_uri='https://api.dailymotion.com/oauth/token'
    )

class MainHandler(webapp.RequestHandler):

  @decorator.oauth_required
  def get(self):

    http = decorator.http()
    resp, content = http.request('https://api.dailymotion.com/me')

    path = os.path.join(os.path.dirname(__file__), 'welcome.html')
    logout = users.create_logout_url('/')
    variables = {
        'content': content,
        'logout': logout
        }
```

```
        self.response.out.write(template.render(path, variables))
    ...
```

If you're looking to implement OAuth 2.0 across a wide variety of services, access your own services with OAuth authorization, or make requests to APIs provided without client libraries, you should consider using an open source library for OAuth 2.0.

Since the specification is still under active development, these libraries each support different versions of the draft specification.

Supporting draft 10, several of the OAuth 2.0 implementations in the Google API client libraries are also available as separate libraries:

- `oauth2client` in Python (*http://code.google.com/p/google-api-python-client/wiki/OAuth2*)
- Google OAuth Client Library for Java (*http://code.google.com/p/google-oauth-java-client/*)

Additional libraries for other languages are available on oauth.net (*http://oauth.net/2/*).

Going Further

In this Getting Started book, we have given you an overview of how OAuth 2.0 works for obtaining authorized access to user data and why it is important to improve security and user productivity. As an application developer, you should now understand the different authorization flows available and how to decide between them when an API provider supports multiple flows. We've also introduced OpenID Connect, discussed how it builds on top of the OAuth 2.0 protocol to enable user authentication, and some of the different security properties of authentication versus authorization. We hope the protocol-level foundation provided by this book will make you a better developer, even if you end up using libraries that abstract many of the details.

As you use OAuth 2.0 in your application, there are additional considerations you should take into account to optimize user experience and performance. When getting access to a user's data, you should explore how requests for different levels of access and the timing of those requests affect approval rates. When authenticating users with OpenID Connect, you should think about which identity providers to support, how you deal with users who have accounts on multiple identity providers, how to improve sign-in performance by decoding the `id_token` JWT, and other potential factors that could decrease customer service tickets.

We primarily focused on the perspective of acting as an OAuth client. Many application developers may wish to open up their data by building OAuth-authorized API resource servers and running their own authorization servers. The knowledge you gained from this book should hopefully make it easier to understand the detailed specifications and security considerations documents that are referenced in the Appendix and are important reading for API providers launching OAuth 2.0 authorized services.

References

While the specifications formed the basis for the description and diagrams of the individual protocol flows, a number of other online resources were used in preparation of this book.

Specifications

- OAuth 2.0 draft (*http://tools.ietf.org/html/draft-ietf-oauth-v2*)
- OAuth 2.0 threat model and security considerations (*http://tools.ietf.org/html/draft-ietf-oauth-v2-threatmodel*)
- OAuth 2.0: Bearer tokens (*http://tools.ietf.org/html/draft-ietf-oauth-v2-bearer*)
- OAuth 2.0: MAC access authentication (*http://tools.ietf.org/html/draft-ietf-oauth-v2-http-mac*)
- OpenID Connect Basic, Standard and Messages (*http://openid.net/connect/*)
- JSON Web Token (JWT) (*http://tools.ietf.org/html/draft-jones-json-web-token*)
- OAuth 2.0: Token revocation (*http://tools.ietf.org/html/draft-lodderstedt-oauth-revocation*)

Vendor Documentation

- Facebook Authentication (*http://developers.facebook.com/docs/authentication/*)
- Facebook Graph API (*http://developers.facebook.com/docs/reference/api/*)
- Digging Deeper into OAuth 2.0 on Force.com (*http://wiki.developerforce.com/page/Digging_Deeper_into_OAuth_2.0_on_Force.com*)
- Authenticating Remote Access with Salesforce (*https://login.salesforce.com/help/doc/en/remoteaccess_authenticate.htm*)
- Google OAuth 2.0 (*http://code.google.com/apis/accounts/docs/OAuth2.html*)
- Google's Internet Identity Research (*https://sites.google.com/site/oauthgoog/*)

- Google's OAuth 2.0 Controllers for iOS (*http://code.google.com/p/gtm-oauth2/wiki/Introduction*)
- OAuth 2.0 on Android (*http://code.google.com/p/google-api-java-client/wiki/Android*)
- OAuth 2.0 on Android with Google Tasks (*http://code.google.com/apis/tasks/articles/oauth-and-tasks-on-android.html*)
- Windows Live SDK—OAuth 2.0 (*http://msdn.microsoft.com/en-us/library/hh243647.aspx*)

Mailing Lists

- OAuth IETF Working Group (*https://www.ietf.org/mailman/listinfo/oauth*)
- OpenID Connect Working Group (*http://lists.openid.net/mailman/listinfo/openid-specs-ab*)
- Google's oauth2-dev forum for questions about their OAuth 2.0 implementation (*https://groups.google.com/forum/#!forum/oauth2-dev*)

Misc

- Google Code blog—OAuth 2.0 changes (*http://googlecode.blogspot.com/2011/10/upcoming-changes-to-oauth-20-endpoint.html*)
- hueniverse blog—OAuth 2.0 (Without Signatures) Is Bad for the Web (*http://hueniverse.com/2010/09/oauth-2-0-without-signatures-is-bad-for-the-web/*)
- OAuth 2.0 flow diagrams (*https://github.com/jricher/OpenID-Connect-Java-Spring-Server/blob/master/docs/OAuth2.0_Diagrams.pdf?raw=true*)

About the Author

Ryan Boyd is a developer advocate at Google focused on enabling developers to extend Google Apps and build businesses on top of Google technology. He previously worked on OpenSocial and led the developer relations team for Google's AtomPub APIs. Prior to joining Google, Ryan worked in higher education as a web architect for RIT's central web hosting environment and as a web app developer building admissions and student systems.

Get even more for your money.

Join the O'Reilly Community, and register the O'Reilly books you own. It's free, and you'll get:

- $4.99 ebook upgrade offer
- 40% upgrade offer on O'Reilly print books
- Membership discounts on books and events
- Free lifetime updates to ebooks and videos
- Multiple ebook formats, DRM FREE
- Participation in the O'Reilly community
- Newsletters
- Account management
- 100% Satisfaction Guarantee

Signing up is easy:

1. **Go to: oreilly.com/go/register**
2. **Create an O'Reilly login.**
3. **Provide your address.**
4. **Register your books.**

Note: English-language books only

To order books online:
oreilly.com/store

For questions about products or an order:
orders@oreilly.com

To sign up to get topic-specific email announcements and/or news about upcoming books, conferences, special offers, and new technologies:
elists@oreilly.com

For technical questions about book content:
booktech@oreilly.com

To submit new book proposals to our editors:
proposals@oreilly.com

O'Reilly books are available in multiple DRM-free ebook formats. For more information:
oreilly.com/ebooks

Spreading the knowledge of innovators   oreilly.com

Have it your way.

O'Reilly eBooks

- Lifetime access to the book when you buy through oreilly.com
- Provided in up to four DRM-free file formats, for use on the devices of your choice: PDF, .epub, Kindle-compatible .mobi, and Android .apk
- Fully searchable, with copy-and-paste and print functionality
- Alerts when files are updated with corrections and additions

oreilly.com/ebooks/

Safari Books Online

- Access the contents and quickly search over 7000 books on technology, business, and certification guides
- Learn from expert video tutorials, and explore thousands of hours of video on technology and design topics
- Download whole books or chapters in PDF format, at no extra cost, to print or read on the go
- Get early access to books as they're being written
- Interact directly with authors of upcoming books
- Save up to 35% on O'Reilly print books

See the complete Safari Library at safari.oreilly.com

 O'REILLY®

Milton Keynes UK
Ingram Content Group UK Ltd.
UKHW051511220824
447250UK00007B/101